Elements of a Prosperous Soul

Keys to a Vibrant Prayer Life

By Lou Federico

Elements of a Prosperous Soul
Copyright © 2007 by Lou Federico
All rights reserved.

This book is protected by the copyright laws of the United States of America. This book may not be copied or reprinted for commercial gain or profit.

Unless otherwise noted, scripture is taken from the Holy Bible, New International Version. Copyright © 1973, 1978, 1984 International Bible Society. Texts are identified by NIV.

New King James Version, Holy Bible © 1982, 1983 by Thomas Nelson, Inc.

God's Word Translation, Holy Bible ©

New Living Translation, Holy Bible ©

King James Translation, Holy Bible ©

ISBN 978-1-4303-1064-8

Cover illustration by Jean Graf and Kevin Frohlich
Tabernacle illustrations by Lou Federico

Special Thanks to those who helped in the publishing of this book in some way:

    Patti Federico
    Alice Quaranta
    Lorraine Bernazzani
    Kevin Frohlich
    Gail Mulligan
    Jean Graf
    Wendy Ginter

Dedications

This book is first dedicated to my wife Patti whose constant encouragement and input I could not do without. She is the love of my life, my partner and my best friend.

To my sons Joshua and Jonathan who make me look good as a father and who are both awesome men of God! Never forget where you've come from in seeking to become all God wants you to be.

I also want to dedicate this book to all those faithful members of Vineyard Community Church in Dutchess County NY. You are my co-laborers in the work of the Lord, and my inspiration to see this work to its completion.

Contents

Preface 9

Chapter 1: The Need for Prayer 13

    Intro 13
    Prayer as a display of humility 14
    Prayer as a weapon of our warfare 18
    Prayer as Intimate Communication with God 23

Chapter 2: Desire for Intimacy 29

    Intro 29
    God's desire to be intimate with us 29
    Our desire for intimacy with God 34
    Walking out intimacy 36

Chapter 3: Praying with Impact 41

    Intro 41
    Unanswered Prayer 42
    Praying according to His will 47
    The role of faith as it applies to prayer 51
    James' Practical Instruction 53

Chapter 4: The Tabernacle of Moses and its Significance to Prayer 59

    Intro 59
    Conception and Purpose 60
    Function and Form 64

Chapter 5: Key #1 A Grateful Heart 71

    Intro 71
    Just Living Life 73
    The Way In 74

Chapter 6: Key #2 Confession 81

    Intro 81
    The Laver and God's Unlimited Mercy 82

  Confessing Sins 87
  Applying, not begging for Forgiveness 89
  Putting it together 91

Chapter 7: Key #3 Reconciliation 93
  Intro 93
  Who is my brother? 100
  As far as it is with you 103
  Putting it together 105

Chapter 8: Key #4 Surrender 107
  Intro 107
  A Sacrifice is Suppose to be Dead 108
  Total Surrender 110
  Putting it together 113

Chapter 9: Key #5 Forgiveness 115
  Intro 115
  Un-forgiveness Equals Bondage 117
  A model for forgiving 124
  Putting it together 129

Chapter 10: Key #6 Confidence 131
  Intro 131
  The Punch Line 134
  Enter Boldly 136
  Entering? Entering What? 136
  Confidence is the key 137
  Putting it together 139

Chapter 11: Key #7 Communication 141
  Intro 141
  Praying to Know the Answer 143
  Times of Refreshing 147
  The role of the Intercessor 150
  Putting it together 151

Chapter 12: Working It In And Out 153
    Intro 153
    Desiring to Desire 155
    Legalism vs. Liberty 157
    Some practical considerations 159

Appendix One 163

Appendix Two 167

Appendix Three 169

Appendix Four 171

Bibliography 175

Preface

I know, I know, I can hear some say, "Not another book on prayer." Well not quite. This book is about more than a prayer life, it is about living a life in right relationship with God and others. When this occurs our soul prospers, and when our soul prospers everything is possible for us. I love how the Lord continually unfolds His promises and purposes to us. His desire *is* that we pray and pray effectively. Hopefully you will be stirred in your heart to pray, but even more than that. I pray that you will find an approach to keep your soul refreshed and in right relationship with God and others.

I have been contemplating this book for some time. The material comes from my own studies and experiences on the topic, and was originally accumulated for the purpose of giving people a practical, everyday model for prayer that would have impact on their lives. It is not meant to be the last word on prayer, nor is it a method or formula to be substituted for intimate and simple relationship with God. It is however, a powerful tool to be used in the context of ones devotional life to bring about refreshing, as well as a means by which you can see things you are praying for positively affected.

As I write, I am assuming a couple of things; First, that my audience is predominantly Christian, and secondly, that you have a value for an intimate relationship with God that includes regular times of being alone with Him. Why are these necessary to the topic at hand? Without knowing Jesus Christ personally, having been filled with His Holy Spirit, the drive, direction, and discernment needed to realize our soul's prosperity through a daily devotional life is futile. Some of this will be apparent as you read on.

The material in this book is not meant to be simply brain food, but a practical application of God's desires for each one of us. *It is what I, and now others, do regularly.* When applied in the midst of ones devotional life, it can be revelatory in accessing the very revival fire many of us so desire, and at the same time a more consistent refreshing of our souls.

I have yet to meet a person who would not want to enhance their prayer life and the awesome sense of God's presence in their daily lives. I do believe that we take some things for granted in our attempts however, and end up frustrated and even defeated. This frustration produces a reluctance to venture back into the realm of intimate communication with God. I also sense that many feel defeated in their prayer lives, constantly wondering why prayers go unanswered. Hopefully, you will find some solutions to the nagging reality of unanswered prayers.

My honest desire is that you come away with a refreshing approach to prayer, and a model, which will serve you daily in your walk with God. The Tabernacle of Moses will be discussed and is used for the purpose of giving you a mental picture of progression. I have purposely avoided getting into the minute details concerning the Tabernacle, its symbolisms and historical significance. If you desire to read more about the Tabernacle of Moses, there are many great authors who do a wonderful job in its description.

Enjoy, but most of all, do it! You will see a marked difference in your prayer life when you do. And remember, the benefits come with continued use, so practice does make perfect. I would also suggest that you read slowly as each chapter can stand alone in benefit to you. You'll be able to assimilate the material much better if you do only one chapter a day.

Chapter 1: The Need for Prayer

Intro

It seems silly to start with a chapter on the need for prayer. Obviously, if you've gotten this far, you must have some inkling of its importance. Unfortunately, I have found people who have been walking with Jesus for many years and yet they do not have a good sense of the need for prayer. At least their actions speak that way. They may say the right things and be able to quote, or at least paraphrase, the right scripture verses and passages on the topic, yet they live as if they never heard them.

I heard a message from a Pastor many years ago, humorously adjuring us on the topic of prayer saying, "What's the point [of prayer]! The Bible says God already knows what you're going to pray before you pray it. (Mat. 6:8) Not only that, He is sovereign over all things, and His purposes will prevail! (Prov. 19:21) So why pray?!" Of course as he continued, he wonderfully expounded on the purpose of prayer and how we were to enter into it.

As a child I can still remember my first solo attempts at prayer. I lived in a home that had a high value for family, church, and tradition, yet prayer was something I perceived as being relegated to a building with a cross in it, or reserved for my bedtime. As I grew up I realized that my perceptions were wrong, and that my mother and others in my family had vibrant prayer lives. At first, prayer to me was a collection of words memorized for the purpose of appeasing this really big God who was up there somewhere. If I wanted to be on His good side He required us to say particular words in the order He gave us to say them. When I did venture into simple conversation with God it was usually on my bed pleading with Him, or His immediate family, not to appear to me that night because He knew I would be too frightened and would die if He did. Prayer had its place, but the reasons I prayed and the motivations behind them were off.

In my conversations with people, I sometimes find that the reasons they pray are similar to that of hedging a bet, or playing a chance game in one of the casinos of Las Vegas. They are looking for a particular thing to happen so to make sure they get it they pull the lever of that "one armed bandit" in the sky and hope for 7's. Prayer to them is impersonal and cold; therefore, the need for it is obscured, tainted, and ultimately ineffective.

Prayer as a display of humility

So what's the point of prayer? The place we will first look may not be that obvious to you. I believe when we delve into the ultimate purposes of God's handiwork in our lives, we *must* come to it however. To me the most important verse in all of the scriptures in understanding a Christian's relationship with God, in conjunction with his/her experiences in this life, is Romans 8:29. I have been known to have people who read the Bible quote for me Romans 8:28 and most can do so.

> "And we know that in all things God works for the good of those who love him, who have been called according to his purpose." (NIV)

Then I ask them to quote for me the next verse, verse 29, and the majority cannot do so.

> "For those God foreknew he also predestined to be conformed to the likeness of his Son, that he might be the firstborn among many brothers." (NIV)

I believe we cannot have a full understanding of Romans 8:28, until we have contemplated the point, which is Romans 8:29. It is as if the two verses should be reversed, with verse 29 coming before verse 28, and in our understanding they need to be.

To say that God knows everything is commensurate with our understanding of who God is. If He doesn't know everything, we are all in trouble. He does, and as the scriptures declare, He knows us, all of us. We are ones who have come into relationship with Him and have been given a deposit, the seal of our salvation within us…the Holy Spirit. The Holy Spirit is the very Spirit of God. This is the same Spirit given to Jesus, empowering Him here on earth. He is what makes a Christian a Christian. More than that, He is the one who leads and guides us through this life. And where is He leading us? To be conformed into the likeness of Jesus. Jesus is our big brother, the model for us all, and everything we do and say is reflected off of Him for quality control purposes. That's why God "...works for good..." things in our lives, because if we truly love Him, His purpose of forming Jesus in us will prevail. We are predestined once we become a Christian. Our direction is set, and it is set in the direction of a Jesus look-a-like!

What does this have to do with prayer? Everything! In Matthew 11:28, Jesus says

"...learn from me, for I am gentle and *humble* in heart..." (NIV)

One of the premiere qualities of Jesus, and a characteristic we are being conformed into, is humility, the humility of Christ. The Bible points out in the book of James, chapter 5, verse 5,

"God opposes the proud but gives grace to the humble." (NIV)

What does that mean?! The Greek word for *opposes* is a combination of two words, *anti* meaning against, and *tasso* meaning to arrange things in order. So when God says He opposes the proud, He is saying that He is against putting things in order for that person. He resists, if you will, the orderly arrangement of things in a person's life. He gives grace however to the humble. Grace in its simplest form means receiving something you don't deserve.

A person who does not pray, who has no need to seek God for His intervention, strength, or answers to life's questions, is basically saying 'I don't need You [God], 'I can do it on my own.' Such an attitude is coming from a proud position, and therefore, one may experience things being out of order in their life. The person who regularly seeks God, the scriptures declare, will find Him, (1Chron. 28:9) and receive the grace of God. They will get what they do not deserve. We don't deserve the kindness and goodness of God, but He freely gives it to us, because He *is* a reward-er of those who diligently seek Him. (Heb. 11:6)

I have two very different friends who typify both these positions. One actually believes that when he prays the very opposite of what he desires occurs, so he doesn't pray. Unwittingly he places himself at the center of his reality, and the universe revolves around him. He is the initiator and cause of his own troubles. His life is "out of order," and it's quite evident to all who know him. I believe it comes from the proud position in his heart toward God. My other friend has a relationship with God that is dependant upon Him and is manifested in his constant outpouring of prayer. This person's faith has brought him through hardships that some would consider too much for one person to bear. Yet his life is "in order." God has aligned his life in such a way that it benefits his family and those around him.

Prayer to me is first and foremost an act of humility. We don't fully understand the interactions between God knowing everything already, including what we are going to pray before we pray it, and His purposes prevailing on the earth no matter what *we* do. Prayer is the means He has chosen to communicate and have a relationship with us. In humility, we come before Him declaring He is sovereign over all, and that He has given us authority in Jesus' name to do the very works of Jesus, even the "greater works." (John 14:12) It's in humility that we come before Him believing that He exists, not only as a reality of person, but in whatever situation we may find ourselves. If we are going to look like, act like, and display Jesus to those around us, we must be people of prayer. Also, if we want to have our lives "in order," in our families, our finances, at work, and in our relationships, we must not be like those who have no need of prayer. We must be in humble agreement with Him who made all things, who knows all things, and who determines all things, according to His own council. He is continually about the task of completing what He started in the first place, and that is forming Jesus in you and me. So we are not to "…kick against the goads…" but we are to humbly submit to His leading and guiding through prayer.

Prayer as a weapon of our warfare

Others have made this analogy before, and it is a good one. The war in the Persian Gulf was an excellent picture of pray at work. Remember how the enemy, the Iraqi's, were dug in and how we, the Americans, were concerned because of the supposed formidable nature of Saddam Hussein's army? Many of us have been in a position of feeling out-gunned, undermanned, and helpless in the face of both natural and spiritual opposition. We know we are in for a fight, but we don't know how to go about calculating our offensive and defensive requirements to win. The Bible says that the battle is the Lord's, and He has given us the means to fight and be victorious.

What we can learn from the Gulf War is that before you send in the ground troops, bomb the enemy by every means possible and as often as possible. Do this by precise use of air attacks, and precession bombing. Prayer is the means we are given to bomb the enemy and pave the way before we venture into anything for the Kingdom of God. When we are involved in ministry of any type, whether to those close to us like family and friends, or those we have yet to meet, prayer must be utilized to ensure total victory.

Living a prayer-less lifestyle is like going onto the fields of Gettysburg as a Confederate Soldier during Picket's Charge, where just about his entire command was lost, under a truly disadvantaged situation. Why? The enemy, in this case the Northern Soldiers, held the high ground. In doing so, they were secure and could shoot down on Picket's men. It became a bloodbath, partly due to the pride of the Confederate Army, and also because they underestimated the enemy, especially the position they held on the battlefield. Our enemy is Satan, and as the Bible declares in Ephesians Chap. 6 verse 12, our

> "...struggle [fight] is not against flesh and blood, but against...the spiritual forces in the heavenly [high] realms [places]."(NIV)(Bracketed additions mine)

If we are to win the day, we must take the high ground, but before we discuss how we do this, let me make sure we don't fall into presumption.

We don't win the fight against the enemy by shaking our fist at the sky and posturing like some little Napoleon. We have been given all authority here on this earth, and the powers that exist have been given permission by God, who is over all, to do so. These Powers are the ones we fight against, but they are not the ones we *pray against*. As a matter of fact, you cannot find prayers prayed in the Bible that "come-against" Principalities or Powers. What you do find are prayers directed toward people and circumstances to positively affect an outcome. We are to be on the offence, taking the high ground, but that is a matter of this earthly plane. As it says in the book of Jude in verses 9 and 10,

> "But even the archangel Michael, when he was disputing with the devil about the body of Moses, did not dare to bring a slanderous accusation against him, but said, "The Lord rebuke you!" Yet these men speak abusively against whatever they do not understand; and what things they do understand by instinct, like unreasoning animals--these are the very things that destroy them." (NIV)

The place of these Powers is a matter of God's plane, the heavenly plane. We have been authorized to do the battle on our plane, the earthly one. The battle we fight on our plane *does* include the casting out of demons, and the "binding of the strongman," but not the casting down of demonic Princes over areas. Praying in such a way is about as effective as a dog barking at the stars in the sky. After he wears himself out from his incessant yelping, the stars still remain. All he succeeds in doing is making himself tired and frustrated, and he eventually gives up. You wouldn't go into an unlit room and shout at the darkness commanding it to go, but you simply turn on the light. We bind the strongman and "come against" the darkness by letting our light, the light of the Holy Spirit, shine through us. The light drives out the darkness.

For us to take the high ground we must be people of prayer. Prayer is the weapon of our warfare by which we unleash the very power of God, who has the ultimate in high ground. The Bible relays an account of the prophet Daniel praying. The prayers he prayed went up to heaven and the answer came via an angel. The angel's progress was hindered however because he came under attack while he was on his way with the answer. (Daniel 10:7–14) His prayers had effect, they ascended to heaven and heaven responded. When Peter was put into prison, some of the believers got together to pray for him. When they did God sent angels to release him. Satan's plan was to use his forces to squash the spreading of the Gospel. He did this through the imprisonment of one of the leaders of the church, but because the believers knew they needed to take the high ground they prayed together. When they did, heaven's answer was unleashed in a supernatural way. (Acts 12:5–11)

Too often I have found well-meaning Christians who have a dualistic view of God's creation. They have a concept of a spiritual battle going on between God and Satan, in which both are in the heavens somewhere entangled in some boxing match, "duking" it out in one big cosmic fight. Unwittingly, they ascribe to Satan co-equal status with God. Beloved, God is in all and over all. No created being, which Satan is, comes even close to the eternal awesome personage of the King of Kings and Lord of Lords. He is the uncreated, all powerful, all knowing, all wise God, who's presence is unmatched, and who's purposes will prevail. Satan, as I like to view him, is but a dog on a leash. He is a big dog with powerful jowls and a loud bark, but under authority, God's authority, nonetheless. He is tolerated only as far he is useful to test and prove men's hearts.

So why are we praying and doing battle against an enemy that is not going anywhere until God says so? He has limited authority to manipulate, lie and attempt to control men's lives through his arsenal of stealing, killing and destroying." (John 10:10) He is the one who entices men to shun and shake their fist at the One True God, to keep them from receiving the free gift of salvation bought for them by the blood of Jesus. We *are* in a battle of two Kingdoms, the Kingdom of God and of Light and the Kingdom of Satan and of Darkness. That battle is a battle for men's souls. The battle is real, the warfare is intense, and we are in the midst of it. Satan wants all men to be like him, formed in his image of rebellion, selfishness, greed and lust. That's why Paul says in his letter to the Romans, Chap. 12,

> "Do not be conformed any longer to the pattern of this world..." (NIV)

The world has been influenced by, and contaminated by, the serpent of the Garden. He is a liar and the father of lies who has duped us into believing his reality and desires for men. He wants to take as many of us with him as possible. It is a war of attrition with a scorched earth policy to destroy what God has created as good. God however, because of His mercy and grace, has given us His Holy Spirit to be with us and live in us. He gives us power and authority over *all* the works of the devil. We are God's answer to Satan's deceptions. We are the secret weapons in the arsenal of the

Kingdom of God. We may look innocent enough, but within us is all the power of God. The same power that raised Jesus from the dead, put armies to flight, and believe it or not, created the universe. Wow! So pray? You bet! God owns the high ground, and if we want to bomb the enemy to soften his grip, we must pray on all occasions with all kinds of prayers.

Prayer as Intimate Communication with God

Someone once told me that God wanted to be intimate and communicate with me. Being from the macho school of education for young boys, with a hunger for the *logical* and rational concepts of life, I didn't get that at first. Prayer for me was more mechanical, and I found myself doing most of the talking. The words *intimate* and *communication* didn't seem to fit my concept of prayer. How can you be intimate with God? The very thought was inconceivable. Communicate? That involves a two-way transmission, with down time in waiting for a response, in other words…listening. Prayer involves listening? If you want to get an answer it does! Why pray if you don't need an answer? Is that being too logical…? I told you so!

It was sometime in that magical year of 1984 that God taught me about intimate communication with Him. Up to that point my prayer life was filled with a lot of me doing all of the talking. More like pleading than talking, because I was not in a good place. I had just come into a relationship with Jesus, that was great, but there was something He wanted to teach me. He wanted me to "be still and know that [He] was God." (Psalm 46:10) I was not in a good place because I was desperate for answers concerning my future. My first wife was leaving me and she was involved with one of my friends. We had just put my father in the hospital, from which he would not return home, with advanced symptoms of Alzheimer's disease, to which he would eventually succumb. So my nice secure world was shaken to its core, and my prayers were filled with a lot of tears and questions until one day when God broke in.

I was in my usual state of grief while praying, when all of a sudden, out of what seemed like the deep recess of my mind, came these words, "O' you of little faith." 'What was that?!' I thought. 'God, is that You? If that is You, I don't recognize Your voice. I only know Your Word through reading the Bible,' I said. I knew that those words were probably in the Bible, but, being such a new believer I didn't know where. So, I prayed again and asked the Lord to confirm what I had heard by showing it to me in the Bible. I simply opened up the Book, looked down and my eyes fell on Matthew 6:25, reading to the end of the chapter.

> "Therefore I tell you, do not worry about your life, what you will eat or drink; or about your body, what you will wear. Is not life more important than food, and the body more important than clothes? ^{26}Look at the birds of the air; they do not sow or reap or store away in barns, and yet your heavenly Father feeds them. Are you not much more valuable than they? ^{27}Who of you by worrying can add a single hour to his life? ^{28}"And why do you worry about clothes? See how the lilies of the field grow. They do not labor or

> spin. ²⁹Yet I tell you that not even Solomon in all his splendor was dressed like one of these. ³⁰If that is how God clothes the grass of the field, which is here today and tomorrow is thrown into the fire, will he not much more clothe you, **O you of little faith**? ³¹So do not worry, saying, 'What shall we eat?' or 'What shall we drink?' or 'What shall we wear?' ³²For the pagans run after all these things, and your heavenly Father knows that you need them. ³³But seek first His kingdom and His righteousness, and all these things will be given to you as well. ³⁴Therefore do not worry about tomorrow, for tomorrow will worry about itself. Each day has enough trouble of its own." (NIV)(Bold is mine)

What a revelation! God is speaking to me! My eyes fell immediately on Matthew 7:7–8,

> "Ask and it will be given to you; seek and you will find; knock and the door will be opened to you. [8]For everyone who asks receives; he who seeks finds; and to him who knocks, the door will be opened." (NIV)

I was not to worry about my future, as I was doing, or worry about what would happen to me, or where I was to go. I was simply to trust the Lord, have faith, and seek Him, and then I would find my answers. This encounter with the living God catapulted me into a new and ever refreshing intimate prayer life. I was to ask, seek Him, knock and keep on knocking until the door was opened to me for whatever it was I needed.

To not pray or give time to intimate communication with the Lord, is to miss out on one of the supreme benefits associated with it. We have the privilege to communicate with God. Imagine if you will, being able to have access to the President of your country, or some other high-ranking official any time you need. What an honor it would be to have such a person as your friend. Your other acquaintances would be climbing all over you to get some insights, just to say they've got the inside scoop, or "I know this from a reliable source."

Prayer is our communication by which we have access to the very power of heaven. It is intimate in that God knows you better than you know yourself. He is your best of best friends. He is closer than a spouse or parent. He made you, and therefore knows everything about you. There is nothing that you do that surprises Him. Are you aware of that? He knows how you will view something when it is presented to you. He knows how you will react when something happens to you. It's not something He is shocked about. The point is…do you know Him that way? 'OH!' You may ask, 'You mean I can?' Of course you can! Does that mean you'll have God all figured out? NO! It does mean that the invitation to be intimate with Him is open, and that He will reveal things to you, you would not otherwise know outside of prayer.

So, intimate communication is a goal in and of itself. Prayer is, or should be, intimate communication. Moses would talk to God "face to face as a man speaks to his friend." (Exodus 33:11) Abraham was called God's friend. Jesus said in John 15:13–15:

> "Greater love has no one than this, that he lay down his life for his friends. 14You are my friends if you do what I command. 15I no longer call you servants, because a servant does not know his master's business. Instead, I have called you friends, for everything that I learned from my Father I have made known to you." (NIV)

He continually makes known to us the will of the Father. Prayer is our link to hearing and knowing God's will for whatever situation we may need. He knows you and wants to communicate with you through prayer.

There is only one thing you need to do for good communication to occur, and that is, BE QUITE. "Be still and know that I am God" is what it says in Psalm 46:10. We need to cease from our constant pleading at times, and look and listen for the answer we so desire. God is a good communicator. The scriptures are full of examples of God's communication with men. We just need to "dial down," as one of my mentors would say, and look for God's response. Intimate communication and prayer go hand in hand, and if we want *to hear* from God, we must be people of prayer.

Chapter 2: Desire for Intimacy

Intro

There is no way I could have a discussion on prayer and not talk about the desire to be intimate. When I say this, I'm not just talking about our desire to be intimate with God, but His desire to be intimate with us as well. The desire for relationship is the theme of all of scripture, and it must be our heart's motivation if we are going to see prayer as a lifetime experience, and not just something that impacts us for the moment.

God's desire to be intimate with us

I love how the Bible points out the fact that it was God who "formed us in our mother's womb." (Psalm 139:13) Having created each of us in a distinct and miraculous manner, it's no wonder the scriptures declare that we are "fearfully and wonderfully made." (Psalm 139:14) Armed with this revelation, we can be confident that God, as our Creator, not only knows us but desires to see His creation completed. He instructs, comforts, and leads us to that which is best. In the book of Mathew, Jesus says "If you, then, though you are evil, know how to give good gifts to your children, how much more will your Father in heaven give good gifts to those who ask Him." (Matt. 7:11) He is saying that if we, as earthly parents know how to love and care for our children, giving them things they sometimes don't deserve, how much more will God our Father, who is infinitely more loving, more kind, who has all wisdom, the perfect parent, know what is best for us.

Starting with the Book of Genesis, God shows Himself as the Father who wants nothing more than to be intimate with His creation. Not only did God speak with Adam and Eve, but it says that He would come and walk in the midst of the garden in the cool of the day. (Genesis 3:8) He just wanted to hang out with them. That's why we see God calling out to them, when He came to the Garden, after they had sinned by eating the apple, looking for them, searching for them, calling them by name. "Adam! Eve! Where are you?" They were hiding because they knew they had listened to "the other guy" instead of their Father. They were embarrassed, and full of guilt, so they hid themselves. Many of us were, and I think sometimes still are, like our forebears. God, the One who created us, is calling out *our* names, desperately looking for us like one looking for children in hiding.

I have used the following illustration many times before, and I believe it to be a good one. We who are parents can get a good sense of God's heart for His children, because we have been faced with not knowing, if just for a moment, where our child might be. For whatever reason, they are out of our sight, or not where we expected them. I can still see my wife running through a store in the mall, literally yelling at the top of her lungs for our son Joshua. She not only had me frantically looking under every clothes rack in the place, but had store employees barring all the exits. There is nothing like a mom in her protective mode. Don't ever get in her way! Jesus, when He was about to enter Jerusalem for the last time, looked at the city and said in Matthew 23:37,

> "O Jerusalem, Jerusalem, you who kill the prophets and stone those sent to you, how often I have longed to gather your children together, as a *hen gathers her chicks* under her wings, but you were not willing." (NIV)(Emphasis mine)

He was giving us a picture of the heart of God. He wanted them to be where He was and to hold them close, even though they had gone off and done stupid things.

With that picture in our minds, it's no wonder we see God doing everything He possibly can to make the way for men to enter into an intimate relationship with Him. Over and over again we see Him saying such things as, "I will be your God and you will be my people." His desires for His creation are clear, 'I want to be with you,' He is saying, and 'I *will* make the way.'

God had Moses make the Tabernacle, a tent where God and Moses could meet while the Israelites traveled through the desert, so that wherever they went, His presence would be with them. The Tabernacle was to be placed in the midst of the people of Israel every time they made camp. He would, in essence, be hanging out with them, just like He did with Adam and Eve in the Garden. It is interesting that when God banned our first parents from the Garden, He placed Cherub Angels, with flaming swords, at its entrance. The entrance to the Garden was on the east side, and that's where He posted His guard. When God directed Moses to build the Tabernacle, He instructed him to place the entrance on the east side. He was giving them a physical picture of His desire to be with them again just as He was before. He was making the way back, and the way back was, if you will, from the east. Back into His presence and back into an intimate relationship with Him.

Once in the Promised Land, Israel's King Solomon built a magnificent Temple that would replace the Tabernacle as God's resting place for His presence with His people. It was to be a more permanent structure since the Israelite nation had been established. The blue prints for the Temple were given to Solomon's father by God, and they were to be followed exactly as He directed. The entrance to the temple, just like the Tabernacle, was from the east. When Solomon was dedicating the Temple, the Lord's presence came and filled it. His presence was so strong, that the priests could no longer perform their ministries. They could only be with God and be surrounded by Him. God our Father was again giving them a physical demonstration of His desires to be with His people.

Jesus' death and resurrection bought more for us than our ticket to heaven. He is Emmanuel, which means, "God with us." God has come down to earth to be with His children, to walk and talk with them. He has come to gather them and bring them safely home to live with Him forever. How can we be with Him now since He has already ascended into heaven? The promise the Father has given us through Jesus is that He would never leave us nor forsake us. He has made good on that promise by coming to us and living with us in the Person of His Holy Spirit. We *are* His Resting Place. We *are* the Temple in which He now resides. God chose Jesus to be born in humble surroundings, to ordinary people, in sub par conditions in a manger. He still chooses to reside in often times broken down, dysfunctional, and frail conditions. Yes, I am talking about you and me. But, just as he redeemed the place of His birth and made it Holy because of His presence in that place, so He does with us. With that, He has made the way for us to share in the most intimate of relationships.

His desire for intimacy has led Him in His magnificent power, grace and humility, to reside forever with His people. He not only can walk and talk with us as He did with Adam and Eve, but He goes where we go and experiences what we experience. He shares in our lives, leading and guiding us as the good Father that He is.

One day, Jesus will come back in physical form. He will set up His Kingdom permanently on earth to live with us forever. We, as a fallen race, will come full circle to the place of our beginnings. To that place where He is our God and we are His people, living together and being cared for by

Him. The New Heavens and New Earth, whose model is the Garden of Eden, will be established. There will be no fear of God, beast, or man, and we will live in intimate relationship with Him forever.

Our desire for intimacy with God

I am concerned that many of us are like the person who says, "Let us live! Let us love! Let us share the deepest secrets of our souls…! You go first." We can be most distrusting sorts. Our experiences in life have led many of us to close up and not be very revealing. As a matter of fact, for some, to be vulnerable in the area of human relationships is to be weak and open to hurt. So…God has gone first. He has already proven His intent. "We love because He first loved us." (1 John 4:19) In experiencing that love, the love of God, there is an awesome and revealing truth. There is nothing on this earth that compares to knowing Him.

I believe that deep inside all of us is this innate desire to know and be known. God has programmed us to be intimate, and most importantly, to desire to be intimate with Him. When we couple this with the fact that He has given us His Holy Spirit, who lives in us and is with us, we have the makings for an explosively Divine experience.

When I first came to know Jesus personally, I was struck with an undeniable truth. God knows me. Not only did He know about me but He knew me like no one else. He knew my thoughts, my feelings, my hopes and dreams, my disappointments, my fears and my sins. That being true, where could I run, where could I hide from Him? I couldn't even hide in my head, in my thoughts, as I was most comfortable in doing. I prided myself on being a person who would not for any reason look bad, even if that meant lying or lying about lying. I could never say I didn't know something or that I had no opinion about something. How embarrassing! "What are you [Louie] ignorant?!" I would actually think that, and thought others were thinking that of me as well. That may sound extreme, but that's what I felt. So much so, that the very first prayer I prayed after being filled with God's magnificent Holy Spirit was, "God, I've been phony all my life, I won't be phony with You." Not that I could be phony with Him in the sense of getting something over on Him. *I* needed to know and say that. How freeing! How liberating! I can now live a life not concerned about what others may or may not think of me, and that's a good thing!

There is, deep inside us all, this desire to be intimate with God. It's not that we have to obtain it somehow; it's already there. Like the boy who told his mother one Christmas he no longer needed his Christmas list. She asked, 'Aren't the toys you wanted on it, and didn't you send your list to Santa already?' 'Yes' he said, 'but I looked in the closet and saw that we already have them.' The desire for intimacy with God is already inside each of us, we just need to open up the closet of our heart and take it out. When we do, the things we thought were just for other people, who we erroneously thought were somehow more spiritual or favored or more gifted or more worthy than we are, becomes our experience in intimate relationship with God. We declare just as the "Beloved" did in the Song of Solomon, "I belong to my lover, and his desire is for me." (SS 7:10)

Walking out intimacy

In walking out intimacy with God, there is one thing we must be, and that is, *intentional*. My good friend, Mr. Webster, defines intentional as the act of doing things on purpose. Too often we forget the old adage; If you aim at nothing you will hit nothing. To have desire for God is not enough, we must do something about it. It is a hunger that must be filled, or we will fill it with something, or worse, someone else. The reality is that nothing else satisfies. That is why God is called El Shaddi, which means, the God who is all-satisfying. As a matter of fact, *He is* Satisfaction Guaranteed!

So how does one walk out intimacy with God? The Bible is full of examples of people walking out an intimate relationship with God. However, instead of looking at them and their lives, because we all are different and living different lives in different circumstances, let's look at one of the ways our relationship with Him is described.

Jesus is called the "Bridegroom" (Matt. 25), and we are called the "Bride." (Rev. 21) How intimate! Just as a marriage between a man and a woman has intimate times, times of sharing, times of drawing near, so we are to spend *time* with our Bridegroom, Jesus.

As a Pastor my all encompassing and oftentimes very revealing question is, 'How are you doing with the Lord?' Not… 'What are you doing for the Lord?' There *is* a difference, but sadly confused for some in living out this life as one of His followers. For many, they are like the church in

Ephesus in the Book of Revelations. (Rev. 2) They were described as a hard working, faithful, and discerning group of people. Not bad! I would like to be called those things. Unfortunately, the thing the Lord had against them was huge, and threatened their relationship with Him. They had forgotten their "first love." The word for "first" here does not necessarily denote *initial*, and is best defined as *priority*. Jesus is supposed to be our priority love. He is first on our priority list. For those of us who use daily planners, our time with Him is to be given "A" status, 'must be done.'

In a marriage, if a couple finds themselves sharing little or no time together, and consequently living two separate lives, we call them "married singles." Yes, they are married, but to look at them you may not realize it. To look at some Christians' lives, we may not realize they have a relationship with the Lord either. Have you ever been at work or at a place where you've gotten to know people over time, and then one day you found out that one of them was a Christian? Seeing that person in that context, saying and doing things they ought not to, especially as a Christian, would make you wonder if they actually had a relationship with the Lord. Their relationship with Jesus, though He is their Bridegroom, is more like "married singles." The benefits of being a couple is found in the time spent with one another. So it is with our relationship with the Lord.

Knowing this, we can see why our parents would warn us about who we hung out with. "Because," they might say, "you are like the company you keep." When people say they are having "quality time" with the Lord, or anyone else for that matter, yet don't spend real time with them, is as if they are saying quantity time is not necessary. To actually have "quality time" in a relationship with Jesus, we must spend quantity time with Him. *You are* like the company you keep. Did you ever notice how couples who spend a lot of time together start to use each other's phrases and mannerisms? Some even start to look like each other! When we begin to spend quantity time with Jesus, He starts to rub off on us, and the "fruit of the Spirit" described in the Book of Galatians (Gal. 5:22), come much more naturally. The fruit of the Spirit belong to the Spirit of God, not to us, and it's not our longevity in the Lord that matters most, but our proximity to Him that means everything. When we try to discipline ourselves only to look like Jesus, our efforts often seem insincere, self-righteous, with no real long term affect. Yet when we are in a relationship with Jesus that is real, intimate and refreshing, we can't help but exude His love, joy, peace and all that He is.

To truly walk out an intimate relationship with God means spending "quality-quantity" time with Him. For some, this may mean setting aside portions of time during the day as a quiet time. For others, it is best described as a "constant communication" with the Lord, knowing He goes everywhere they do. I like to look at it as both, because that is what I see Jesus doing when He physically walked here on this earth. In the Gospels, we see Jesus going off on His own or getting up early in the morning before everyone else to spend time in prayer with His Father (Mark 1:35). We also see Him, while teaching and caring for people, in constant communication with His Father (Matt. 11:25). His intimate relationship was not left in His "prayer closet," it was who He was.

I, like many others before me who venture into the topic of prayer, seem to be drawn to that fateful night in the Garden of Gethsemane (Mark 14:32) when Jesus, in His most desperate of hours, calls His intimate earthly friends to be with Him to stand, watch and pray. What does He find, and what do they come to realize? They couldn't do it for just one hour. One hour was all He was looking for, and because of life's happenings, they were tired and couldn't stay awake. He even tried to get them to look at it from a selfish point of view, for something they could get out of it. He told them that if they would watch and pray with Him, they would not fall into temptation. (Mark 14:38) In other words, if they would spend some quality-quantity time with Him, they wouldn't get into the things the devil was trying to put on them. They would neither have the time nor the desire for anything else but for the One who truly satisfies…Jesus.

There is what I call "bulls-eyes" in my life. One of them is to spend at least one hour a day alone with Jesus. Sometimes I get there, sometimes I don't, but it remains the thing I aim for in my personal walk with Him. This I know…when I do, and I do it on a consistent basis, the things promised to me in scripture I realize. Temptation loses its grip. The love, joy and peace associated with the Spirit of God, along with all the other "fruit of the Spirit" are evident, and not only to me, but to those around me as well. A famous classical musician once said, "When I don't practice one day, I notice. When I don't practice two days, my instructor notices. When I don't practice three days, my audience knows it." So it is with walking in intimate relationship with Jesus. When I don't spend one day with the Lord, I notice, when I don't spend a couple of days with the Lord, those closest to me notice. If for some reason I let my personal time with Him lapse for an extended period of time, everyone notices!

If you are someone who has caught the desire to be intimate with Jesus, and you want to know more about how to spend an hour alone with Him, yet you don't know where to start, see the appendix of this book, where you will find a section called, "The Fifteen Minute Hour." It will help you, as it did me, to fulfill Jesus' call to watch and pray with Him for one hour. Use it to get started, and when you don't need it anymore, and can say 'One hour?! One hour is not enough time to spend with my Savior, I need more!' Then you'll be in the midst of experiencing what the scripture promises, "…times of refreshing…" (Acts 3:19) You will be refreshed, your soul will prosper, and you will be refreshing to those around you.

Chapter 3: Praying with Impact

Intro

Have you ever felt as if your prayers made it as far as your chin, and then simply dropped to the floor? I have, and a lot of what I am sharing in this book stems from my own experiences in what I have concluded as "ineffective" praying. No matter how much I tried to force my prayers to heaven, I couldn't get them there any better.

Let's make something perfectly clear right from the start; God hears our prayers…period! He is not deaf. He *is* attentive to your cries. The very first Scripture I put to memory after my salvation experience speaks of His attention to us. Psalm 116:1–2 says,

> "I love the Lord, because he has heard my voice and my supplications. Because He inclined his ear to me, therefore I will call on Him as long as I live." (NRSV)

God heard me cry out to Him even when I didn't deserve to be heard. How wonderful is the grace of God!

In this chapter, we will look at what hinders our prayers. We will also look at how we can guarantee receiving what we ask for in prayer and how we can make our prayers something of impact. I know that sounds like a bold statement, I thought so too when I first read it...in the Bible. Yes, Jesus said it first. Doesn't He always!? We are copycats... commentators on an already revealed truth which *God* has made known. There is however, a way to help us filter out the grain from the chaff, the substance from the fluff, pearls from the mass of others things that just look good. In other words, there is a place from which our prayers have a greater impact, and there *are* prayers we know are always His will.

Unanswered Prayer

"When Norman Vincent Peale was a boy, he found a big black cigar. He slipped into an alley, and lit up. It didn't taste good, but it made him feel very grown-up...until he saw his father coming. Quickly he put the cigar behind his back and tried to be casual. Desperate to divert his father's attention, Norman pointed to a billboard advertising the circus. 'Can I go, Dad? Please, let's go when it comes to town.' His father's reply taught Norman a lesson he never forgot. 'Son', he answered quietly but firmly, 'never make a petition while at the same time trying to hide a smoldering disobedience.[1]'" How poignant, and how much to the point.

For most Christians the question inevitably comes, "Why do my prayers go unanswered?" One reason is simple...the "smoldering disobedience," otherwise known as sin. As a friend of mine was fond of saying, "the problem is not on God's end." Sin truly does separate us from God. You know the Scripture in Romans 8:38-39,

> "For I am convinced that neither death nor life, neither angels nor demons, neither the present nor the future, nor any powers, neither height nor depth, nor anything else in all creation, will be able to separate us from the love of God that is in Christ Jesus, our Lord." (NIV)

Unfortunately sin can separate us from God. Not from His Love for us, that remains a constant. Our right standing with Him however is compromised. In Psalm 66:18, King David writes,

> "If I had cherished sin in my heart, the Lord would not have listened." (NIV)

Things like pride and un-forgiveness act as barriers to God's answer to prayer. Jesus said if we do not forgive, God cannot forgive us (Matt. 6:15). Both James and Peter state that God opposes or resists the proud (James 4:6; Peter 5:5). The things God would like to do for us are hindered by our sin. They act as umbrellas keeping us from the "reign" of His Kingdom over our lives, and in particular, the things we are praying for. In reference to prayers that go unanswered, Peter says that a man's prayers are hindered if he does not honor/respect his wife. (1 Peter 3:7) Why? Because we are to treat our wives as Jesus does the church, and anything that does not reflect Jesus is sin.

The Scriptures declare in 2 Cor. 5:21,

> "God made him who had no sin to be sin for us, so that in Him we might become the righteousness of God. (NIV)

Jesus took our punishment for us by His death on the cross and as a result we are now "positional-ly" righteous. We are the righteousness of Christ. That is one reason I believe that at the time of salvation, when a person comes to faith in Jesus Christ through the Holy Spirit, they experience a closeness to Him they later mark as the highlight of their Christian lives. This "honeymoon period", as some have described it, was a result of having every sin they had committed wiped away in an instant, and their hearts were overwhelmed by the Love of God. This closeness to the Lord is striking, with seemingly every "Fruit of the Spirit" in operation right from the beginning.

I understand the traditional teaching concerning the "Fruit of the Spirit" as being something that happens over time. This teaching says something like, 'the roots must go deep, and the tree must mature for it to produce ripe fruit.' This teaching of course suggests that time is needed. I believe there is another way of looking at it.

Have you ever met "older" Christians who would boast about being "with the Lord over twenty years," and looking like they had never met Him? I have, and it can be a little embarrassing. Then there are those Christians you meet who are just days or weeks old in the Lord and they are oozing Jesus everywhere. I believe it's not ones' longevity in the Lord that matters most, its ones' proximity to Him. It's how close you are to Him right now, not just in "positional" righteousness but "experiential" righteousness as well. The "Fruit of the Spirit" are truly that, the fruits *of the Spirit* of God. They belong to Him, and they are manifested through us as we walk in intimacy with Him, confessing our sins, appropriating His forgiveness, and being conformed into His likeness.

1 John 1:9 says,

"If we confess our sins, He is faithful and just to forgive us our sins and to cleanse us from all unrighteousness." (NKJV)

This was written to Christians, not to those who did not have the Holy Spirit of God living in them. Sinning equals unrighteousness, or living a life outside a right standing with God. Sin separates us from God and can certainly hinder our prayers.

Sin is not the only reason why prayers go unanswered however. Did you know that the Apostle Paul, the one who wrote one-third of the New Testament, had prayer go unanswered? In 2 Corinthians 12:7–12 Paul says he "pleaded with the Lord," in other words prayed, "three times" that what he called a "thorn in the flesh" would be taken away. God spoke to Him gently and told Him that His "grace [was] sufficient for [him]," but the answer was essentially, 'No.' Why? Because, as Paul says, "To keep him from becoming conceited." Conceited?! The Apostle Paul?! Never! Oh yes, and it can happen to the best of us. There was a higher calling for Paul, as with all of us, and that is Christ-likeness. God knew Paul, and Paul knew himself. He, like us, needed to know and experience dependence upon God as our only choice. It is the "weakness" Paul is referring to in this passage of scripture. "Pride comes before the fall" (Pr.16:18). He didn't want that for Paul and He doesn't want that for us either. The grace given to us through answered prayer must never be taken for granted. We get what we get because of His grace and mercy, not because we are so wonderful, or our vocal inflections are just right. He is able and we are not. That's why we pray in the first place. God loved Paul too much to allow the great things He was showing him to cause Paul to think of himself more highly than he ought. If Paul was allowed to do that God would have to humble him, and He was saving him from that embarrassment.

Jesus gave us the right attitude toward prayer in Matthew 26:39. In His most desperate hour in the Garden of Gethsemane He cried out,

> "My father, if it is possible, may this cup be taken from me. Yet not as I will but as you will." (NIV)

The ultimate will of God must always be our consideration when there seems to be unanswered prayer in our lives. Sometimes, the things we desire and ask for in prayer just go against what God wants to have happen. I'm sure there were sincere Christian people who were "loyalists" during the time of the American Revolution, praying as fervently as the Revolutionaries for God to favor their side. Yet I believe it was God's will and favor that established the United States.

I can hear many saying, "You know Lou, "No" *is* an answer to prayer, so why are you saying the prayer is going unanswered." Of course there are three possibilities when expecting an answer: "Yes", "no" or "not yet," but when we pray we should fully expect what we ask for in prayer (Mark 11:24). That is called faith. So when we do not realize a positive response to our petition, the prayer is essentially "unanswered." We didn't get what we asked for.

This book is not about why our prayers go unanswered however, but how we can become more effective in prayer by maintaining a prosperous soul. So the best parts are yet to come.

Praying according to His will

In 1 John 5:14–15 Paul writes,

"This is the confidence we have in approaching God: that if we ask anything according to his will, he hears us. [15] And if we know that he hears us—whatever we ask—we know that we have what we asked of him." (NIV)

Paul is saying that there is a place we can be confident in coming near God with our prayers and petitions, knowing that they will be answered in the affirmative. That place is where our intimate communication with God and "His will" come together. The first half of this equation we have already spoken of in previous chapters. So how can we know His will and pray it back to Him?

God's Will has been a topic of conversation between Christians and their pastors forever. Everyone wants to know the answer to this question, especially as it relates to their own lives. Deep down we all want to get it right. So how can I know God's will for me? Unfortunately, that's not as easy as we would sometimes hope. However, prayer is the vehicle God has afforded us to get the answers we so desire, and there are prayers we can pray that are always His will. For instance, to seek the Lord for what He would have you do with your life, *is* praying according to His will. Why? Psalm 16:11 says,

> "You will show me the way of life, granting me the joy of your presence and the pleasures of living with you forever." (NLT)

God's desire is to direct us in the way of life. The Bible also says, in Deut. 4:29,

> "But if from there you seek the Lord your God, you will find him if you look for him with all your heart and with all your soul." (NIV)

Moses spoke this to the Israelites when warning them about falling away from God, and then later praying to Him for help. The promise is, "you will find Him." You will! As a matter of fact, He will make the answer obvious to you. You won't have to look for some mystical interpretation of circumstances that you're not sure of, which may bring some level of confusion.

Too often I find Christian people who are praying for something, and so desperate for an answer, that they look to every little thing that happens around them as the answer to that prayer. They try to piece together small bits of circumstances into a single interpretation, which oftentimes reflects their already conceived deepest expectations. God is bigger then all of that! He is able to make the answers to our prayers so absolutely plain. It's only our impatience that so often gets in our way to truly hearing from God. That is why I appreciate Psalm 27 so much. In it King David is pouring out his heart concerning his faith and confidence to hear from God when he seeks Him. What is David's advice in the last verse of the Psalm?

> "Wait for the Lord, be strong and take heart and wait for the Lord." (NIV)

God will let us go ahead of Him if we want, and that's scary. God will make the answer to our prayer obvious to us if we wait and it's only our own impatient desires that we run ahead of the answer, or sadly, even make it up by trying to piece together circumstances into a response which later proves *not* to be God. I've had to listen to people as they voiced their frustration at God, wondering why He would lead them into the confusing situation they found themselves. The problem is He hadn't led them there. They led themselves there.

The good news is that God is for us and not against us. You see, even if we are like the Israelites, and find ourselves someplace we are not supposed to be, He will deliver us as we seek Him with our whole heart and soul. In other words, a heart that does not have a preconceived notion of what God's answer or direction will be. It is a heart that is so devoted to Him that there are no idols which discretely dictate our actions and responses.

1 John 5:14 says,

> "This is the confidence we have in approaching God: that if we ask anything according to his will, he hears us." (NIV)

Do you want to pray according to His will? Let's look at some of the things God always answers because *they are* His will: (Please note this is not meant to be an exhaustive list.)

> -*Your cry for help* (Psalm 50:15, 145:19; Isaiah 30:19, 58:9)
>
> -*Needs of the poor* (Psalm 33:18–19, 72:12; Isaiah 41:17)
>
> -*For His Kingdom to come* (Matthew 6:10)
>
> -*For your own salvation* (Psalm 91:14–16; John 17:20; Acts 16:31)
>
> -*For the salvation of others* (2 Chronicles 7:14; Acts 16:31)
>
> -*For the in-filling of the Holy Spirit* (Luke 11:13)
>
> -*For His provision* (Matthew 6:11)
>
> -*For forgiveness* (Matthew 6:12; 1 John 1:9)
>
> -*For wisdom* (James 1:5)
>
> -*For unity of the Body of Christ* (John 17:21)
>
> -*Protection from the Evil One* (Matthew 6:13; John 17:15)
>
> -*To know His will* (Matthew 6:10; Romans 12:2)

There is an obvious truth that is revealed as we look at this list. There is no mention of the house you're looking to buy, or the trip you're about to take, or even the job you're presently employed to do. However, the means to ascertain the direction you are looking for is available to you. There is a great amount of liberty in the Lord, much more than we realize at times. When you said "Lord I give you my life", He took it. What does that mean? It means your Heavenly Father is always directing you and the circumstances in your life for your benefit. You are where you are supposed to be, and it's not what happens to you that matters most, it's what you do with what happens to you. God uses all the things in our lives for our good and to make us more like His Son. That's called faith.

The role of faith as it applies to prayer

We cannot leave this section without mentioning the role of faith as it applies to prayer. Jesus said in Mark 11:24,

> "Therefore I tell you, whatever you ask for in prayer, believe that you have received it, and it will be yours." (NIV)

James the Lord's brother said in James 5:14,

> "And the prayer offered in faith will make the sick person well; the Lord will raise him up. If he has sinned, he will be forgiven." (NIV)

So what does faith have to do with prayer? Everything! If we have faith enough to go to God in prayer yet we don't have faith in Him to answer that prayer, we are what the Bible calls "double-minded." James 1:5–8 says,

> "If any of you lacks wisdom, he should ask God, who gives generously to all without finding fault, and it will be given to him. [6] *But when he asks, he must*

believe and not doubt, because he who doubts is like a wave of the sea, blown and tossed by the wind. [7] That man should not think he will receive anything from the Lord; [8] he is a double-minded man, unstable in all he does." (NIV)(Emphasis mine)

That would be a shame wouldn't it? It's like a man who is dying of thirst, his throat is parched, his lungs are burning, and all the while a canteen full of water is strapped to his belt. As Christian people we have what we need. The water, if you will, is in us. We have all that we need and it resides with the Holy Spirit of God.

When Jesus cursed the fig tree and it subsequently died, Peter was amazed at the dramatic and immediate response to Jesus' prayer of command (Mat. 21:18–22). It is that which prompted Him to say simply "believe." "Have faith in God," is what He says in Mark's Gospel. Hey, it's not about you anyway. It is about Him who lives in you, and He said there is a place where you can have confidence, knowing that you are praying according to His will. So go for the gusto! What do you have to lose? God is for you and not against you.

Faith is the issue, and when it is exercised the results are awesome. "There was a little nun who was on a much desired mission assignment to the Apache Indians. She was so excited that she drove past the last gas station without noticing that she needed gas. She ran out of gas about a mile down the road, and had to walk back to the station. The attendant told her he would like to help her, but he had no container to hold the gas. Sympathetic to her plight, he agreed to search through an old shed in the back for something that might suffice. The only container that would hold fuel was an old bedpan. The grateful nun told him that the bedpan would work just fine. She carried the gasoline back to her car, taking care not to drop an ounce. When she got to her car, she carefully poured the contents of the bedpan into the tank. A truck driver pulled alongside the car as the nun was emptying the container. He rolled down his window and yelled to her, 'I wish I had your faith, sister.²'"

What is the point of that illustration you may ask? People are looking for someone to exercise faith, and just believe God for the impossible. And if we can move mountains, then there is nothing that cannot happen through faith in Jesus. Plus, I just love that story, and I had to find a place for it somewhere!

James' Practical Instruction

The title of this chapter is "Praying with Impact," and I can think of no better place to understand this than the book of James. Being of Italian descent, I just love James. He's so practical, and Italians love that. You know..., 'Greeks speak philosophy and Romans build roads.' In speaking of prayer James writes in James 5:16,

> "Therefore confess your sins to each other and pray for each other so that you may be healed. The prayer of a righteous man is powerful and effective." (NIV)

What he is saying is that there is sin in our lives, and *it does* affect our prayers. Be smart and confess them to each other.' Why should we do this? I believe so that the enemy, Satan, has no foothold. He operates in darkness but God is Light, and as His children we are to operate in the light. So don't keep sin to yourself, in the dark, confess it to someone you trust and bring it to light. In this way the enemy will be given no foothold and the person you confess to can pray for you. In another translation in the Bible, it says it this way,

> "…the effective, fervent prayer of a righteous man avails much." (NKJV)

This is what we want to focus on. The Greek word for "effective/fervent" is "energeo" the word we get "energy" from. It means: active, efficient, mighty. It comes from two words which literally mean: to toil. The Greek word for prayer here is "deesis," which means: to petition, to beg or to supplicate. In combining these words we get the picture of someone really going after what they want with all their heart. Interestingly, James in just six short verses refers to prayer seven times. He wanted to make sure we understood the importance of what he was describing. As a person with the reputation for being faithful in prayer, it is said that James acquired the nickname "old camel knees." Do you think he knew and experienced what he was sharing with us? Absolutely!

Whose prayer does he say is effective? It is the prayer "of a righteous man." Actually, there is no word "man" in the original text here, so a better rendering would be "of a righteous one." A righteous one by definition is someone whose life is equitable and in right order, someone who is innocent and holy. If you haven't picked it up by now, there is a problem, and the question must be asked, Innocent…Holy…Me? No chance!

The Bible speaks of righteousness in two ways; what I call "positional righteousness" and "experiential righteousness". We are *positional-ly* righteous because of our relationship with Jesus. He has made us that way. Romans 3:21–22 (NIV) says,

> "But now a righteousness from God, apart from law, has been made known, to which the Law and the Prophets testify. [22] This righteousness from God comes through faith in Jesus Christ to all who believe. There is no difference…" (NIV)

Also, in 2 Corinthians 5:21(NIV), Paul writes:
> "God made him who had no sin to be sin for us, so that in him we might become the righteousness of God." (NIV)

In other words, as a follower of Jesus, one of the elect of God, you *are* righteous, and it has nothing to do with the law, the do's and don'ts, it comes from Him. You are righteous because He is righteous and you are in Him. That's some more GOOD NEWS!

However, even though we *may know* this to be true we don't always act that way and subsequently, and very importantly, feel that way. This is where "experiential righteousness" comes in. Paul aptly describes this in Romans 7:23–25,

> "I see another law at work in the members of my body, waging war against the law *of my mind* and making me a prisoner of the law of sin at work within my members. [24] What a wretched man I am! Who will rescue me from this body of death? [25] Thanks

> be to God—through Jesus Christ our Lord! So then, I myself *in my mind* am a slave to God's law, but in the sinful nature a slave to the law of sin." (NIV)(Emphasis mine)

So he says in Ephesians 6:14,

> "Stand firm then, with the belt of truth buckled around your waist, with the breastplate of righteousness in place..." (NIV)

What is the truth? Yes, we do sin, but He has saved us from sin and its condemnation. We must stand firm in the parallel truths of what the Apostle John taught us regarding the teachings of Jesus in 1 John 1:9-10,

> "If we confess our sins, he is faithful and just to forgive us our sins, and to cleanse us from all unrighteousness. [10] If we say that we have not sinned, we make him a liar, and his word is not in us." (NIV)

As believers, we still fall short. We still miss the mark of reflecting who Jesus truly is in reality, and that's our sin. *Our experience does not match our position*, and so there is a "war waging" in our minds. The way we make sure this does not affect our hearts is with the breastplate of *experiencing* righteousness through the blood of Jesus, by which we are cleansed again and again. Sin *does* separate us from God, and therefore, our prayers can be hindered. That's why James, though speaking to believers and knowing they are "positional-ly righteous," emphasizes the fact that the "prayer of a righteous [one]", one who stands before God cleansed from all unrighteousness, are "powerful and effective."

God knows what we are going to say before we say it. He hears the cries of the unregenerate, so it's not that he doesn't hear you or will not answer you. The Bible says your prayers are hindered. Look again with me at 1 Peter 3:7,

> "Husbands, in the same way be considerate as you live with your wives, and treat them with respect as the weaker partner and as heirs with you of the gracious gift of life, so that nothing will *hinder your prayers.*" (NIV)(Emphasis mine)

For a husband not to be considerate and respectful to his wife is sin, it does not reflect who Jesus is, and as such that husband's prayers can be hindered, or by definition, "chopped out." As was also pointed out earlier, Jesus said in Matthew 6:15,

> "But if you do not forgive men their sins, your Father will not forgive your sins." (NIV)

Wow! Un-forgiveness is a sin, and as such separates us from God, and in that state, our prayers can be hindered, specifically in asking for forgiveness for ourselves.

So James is saying, one who is righteous, in right standing with God, innocent and holy, that "one's" prayers do something really big! What do they do? They "avail much" (NKJV), they are powerful and effective (NIV), they "can accomplish much." (NSAB) In the original language it could be put this way; *the prayer is strong enough. It's healthy and able. It is a can do prayer which will work. It will have energy to be better, more earnest, and do more than it would have if it weren't coming from a place of righteousness.* This is the place where Mark 11:23 type prayers are prayed and answered.

> "I tell you the truth, if anyone says to this mountain, 'Go, throw yourself into the sea,' and does not doubt in his heart but believes that what he says will happen, it will be done for him. [24] Therefore I tell you, whatever you ask for in prayer, believe that you have received it, and it will be yours." (NIV)

Praying prayers of impact are what you and I need. So don't be caught napping like the disciples in the Garden of Gethsemane. Time is short, both yours and the world's, so there's no time to waste.

Chapter 4: The Tabernacle of Moses and its Significance to Prayer

Intro

The Bible is full of symbols. New Christians often ask me how the Old Testament relates to their lives as believers in Jesus. Of course the answer is, "Jesus is all over the Old Testament." The things laid down by God in its laws and ceremonies not only have found their fulfillment in Christ but even give us a clearer understand of Him. Such is the case with the Tabernacle.

My intent is not to go into every detail concerning the Tabernacle. However, a brief synopsis is appropriate so that you will be able to have a better understanding of your own relationship to God in prayer. The chapters following this one will give you a model for prayer that will use the Tabernacle as its base. Therefore we must delve into its significance as it relates to prayer and a prospering soul.

Conception and Purpose

Did you ever need a focal point in your life? Those of us who have had children and have gone through Lamas classes know something about focal points. The focal point was that spot on the wall or that picture we brought with us for the one in labor to stare at to get through it all. For my wife, it was my face as I attempted to breathe with her without passing out. The Tabernacle was something like that. It was at the center of the Israelite community as they traveled to the Promised Land. It was with them as they walked through the desert, while they vanquished their foes, saw miracles happen, and even when they were being tested by God. When the Tabernacle was set up, all the tribes of Israel encamped around it. A pillar of fire hovered over it during the night, and in the day a cloud did the same, to represent God's presence as Israel's true leader. The Tabernacle became the focal point of worship, direction, and community.

God told Moses in Exodus 25:8–9,

"Then have them [the Israelites] make a sanctuary for me, and I will dwell among them. Make this tabernacle and all its furnishings exactly like the pattern I will show you." (NIV)(Insert mine)

God wanted to "dwell" with His people. He wanted to hang out with them. It is what He's always wanted… relationship with His creation. He made the first move, they didn't! God is always making the first move, and the Tabernacle was His way, at that time, to lead and be among His people.

In his book "Portraits of Christ in the Tabernacle" Theodore H. Epp says that the Tabernacle had three distinct purposes; First, for God "to dwell in the midst of Israel[1]," second "to teach men the holiness of God[2]" [while showing them] the sinfulness of mankind, and third to "show sinful man the only way to salvation[3]."

Epp points out various ways in which God has progressively shown himself to dwell with man throughout history. Starting with Adam and Eve in the Garden of Eden, and culminating with the indwelling of the Holy Spirit in every follower of Jesus, God has continually made a way to be with His people. He always finds a way, and aren't we glad we live at the time when we can say "God lives in me!" Now that's exciting and refreshing. Our experience with the living God is personal and immediate. We don't have to go somewhere or do something to be in His presence. He is with us all the time!

God used the Tabernacle as a way to accomplish His desire to dwell among His people. According to Epp, He also used it to reveal His holiness and man's sinfulness. The Tabernacle represented, in the way it was constructed, the separation between God and man. First, there was the curtain that surrounded the entire compound, separating the Israelites in their encampment from the way into the place where He dwelt inside the Tabernacle. This separation was significant in that it represented God's holiness as transcending the base things of life. Not that God is disinterested or inactive in our lives, but outside of them and not subject to them. Second, there was the "Tent of Meeting" or the "Tabernacle Proper," where only the priests could go to fulfill the ordinances laid down by God for worship inside it. This priestly class was a group anointed and instructed by

God Himself to intercede on behalf of the people. Interestingly, as followers of Jesus *we* now are the priests. We are, as the scriptures declare, a "royal priesthood…a holy nation." (1 Peter 2:9) Lastly, there was the "Holy of Holies" which was further separated inside the Tent of Meeting by a curtain which only Moses and a few others could enter. This is where God's presence dwelt and where Moses would speak with God face to face.

Jesus' death on the cross tore the curtain separating the "Holy of Holies" from all those serving and worshipping God. At the death of Jesus on the Cross Luke the Gospel writer declares, in Luke 23:45,

> "…for the sun stopped shining. And the curtain of the temple was torn in two." (NIV)

Now all can enter freely into His presence without hindrance. We are those who not only worship God, but know Him intimately. We are welcome, as Moses was, into the very presence of the King of all creation.

There wasn't a doubt in the mind of the ordinary Israelites that they were separated from God. God was over there and they were over here, and the reason was because they were not holy enough. In other words they were sinful and could not enter into the immediate presence of God. An intermediary and sacrifice was required on behalf of the ordinary Israelite. Otherwise s/he was out of luck.

As one of the ordinary, as we all are, how wonderful to know that because of the sacrifice of Jesus on the Cross, there is no longer any separation between God and man. We now just simply appropriate to ourselves the salvation purchased for us by our Savior in making Him the Lord over our lives.

This brings us to the key purpose of the Tabernacle according to Epp, and that was, "to emphasize…that they [the Israelites] could approach God in only one way, by means of a blood sacrifice.[4]" In Leviticus 17:11c it says,

> "…it is the blood that makes atonement for one's life." (NIV)

The word "atonement" means to cover over, cancel or forgive. Forgiveness could only be acquired through the shedding of blood which was used to atone for the sins of the people. That's why God killed an animal to make coverings, skin outfits, for Adam and Eve when they disobeyed Him. From that time blood was required. Why? Because, as it says in Leviticus 17:11a,

> "For the life of the flesh is in the blood." (NIV)

For us to live physically we need blood to be flowing through our veins and arteries. For us to live spiritually, where we truly live as spiritual beings, blood is required by a just God to atone for the transgressions of man. What we do physically affects us spiritually and what we do spiritually affects us physically. Sin is a spiritual disease which is made manifest in the emotional *and* physical realms. Jesus shed His blood for us so that we wouldn't have to shed ours. His sacrifice for us in the physical realm has consequences for our salvation in the spiritual realm, the realm of the soul, as well as in nature. It is a complete salvation affecting our whole person, spirit, soul and body. That's Good News!

What does all this have to do with prayer? The Tabernacle was built as a great communication complex. It was the place where a direct link was established between heaven and earth, between God and man, with all the different structures and items in it acting as circuits through which the signal must pass for a clear channel.

Function and Form

There was a progressive nature to the placement and use of the main parts within the Tabernacle. For identification purposes we will define them as: *The Gate*, or entry way into the Tabernacle Courtyard, *The Altar* and *The Laver*, both of which were in the Courtyard. *The Holy Place* and the *Most Holy Place* (Holy of Holies) were in the "Tent of Meeting." (Fig. #1)

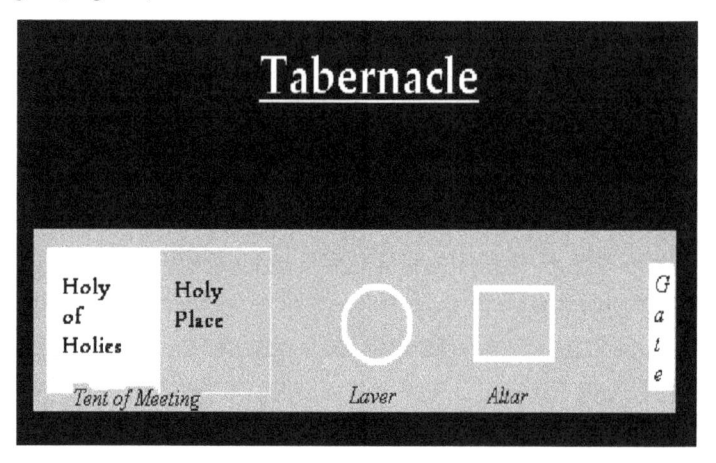

(Figure #1 - The Layout and placement of items inside the Tabernacle)

When the priest would enter the Tabernacle he would go through the only gate that was available. As Christians, we know that there is only one way by which we must come to God, and that is through Jesus Christ. Jesus said in John 10:9,

> "I am the gate; whoever enters through me will be saved. He will come in and go out, and find pasture." (NIV)

Also, the way in which the Tabernacle was positioned each time it was set up, was with the Gate on the East side. Two things are appropriate to us in this: First, when Adam and Eve were cast out of the Garden of Eden, the place where they had relationship with God, walked with Him and were in His presence, Cherubim were placed on the East to guard it from further entry (Genesis 3:24). So, the way back into His presence, if you will, is from the East. Second, when God gave Moses instructions about how the Tabernacle was to be positioned and where each tribe of Israel was to camp around it, He placed the tribe of Judah on the East.

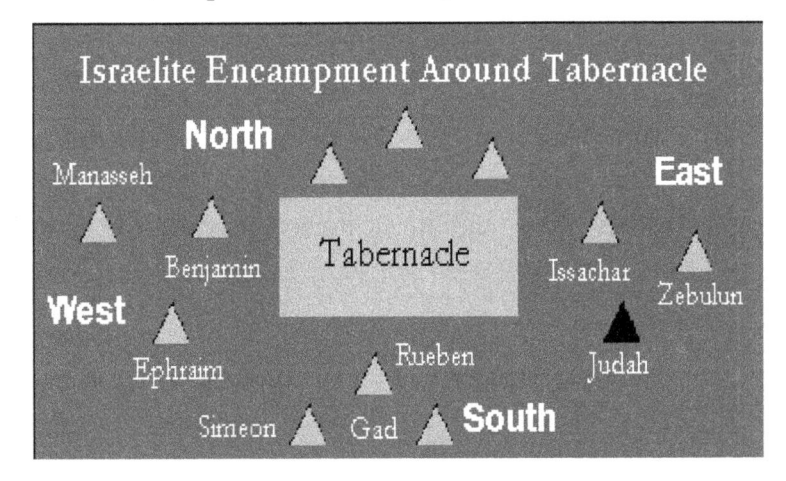

(Figure #2 – The Tribes of Israel encamped around the Tabernacle)

Jesus is called the Lion of the Tribe of Judah, and as the Messiah of God, prophetically declared to come from the East. (Ezekiel 43:2-4, Revelation 5:5) (Fig. #2) The Magi as well came from the East, and of course that is where Jesus' Star was positioned for them to follow. (Matthew 2:1-2)

Upon entering the Tabernacle, the first thing the priests would see would be the Altar of Sacrifice where offerings were made. (Fig. #1) It was used to make the daily sacrifices necessary for the proper worship of God as prescribed by Moses. The blood of animals was used to atone for the sins of the people. Jesus is our sacrificial Lamb, and His sacrifice is the first thing we must recognize on our way to the presence of God.

The Laver was actually the first place the priest would go before making sacrifices at the Altar. He would wash his hands and feet there as a symbol of cleansing. Interestingly, the Laver was the only item within the Tabernacle that had no dimensions. It represents the unlimited nature of God's forgiveness.

Within the Tent of Meeting, an actual tent type structure, were the Holy Place and the Holy of Holies. The Holy Place had three items in it; the Menorah or Lamp Stand, the Table of Showbread, and the Altar of Incense.

The Lampstand gave light to those ministering inside the Holy Place and stood on the priests' left. The Table of Showbread had twelve loaves on it representing the Twelve Tribes, the people of God, and stood on the right.

The Altar of Incense, where the priest would offer up prayers on behalf of the people was straight ahead, and was in front of the curtain separating the priest from the Most Holy Place, or Holy of Holies.

Tabernacle and Tent of Meeting

Ark of the Covenant · Table of Showbread · Altar of Incense · Lampstand

Holy of Holies **Holy Place**

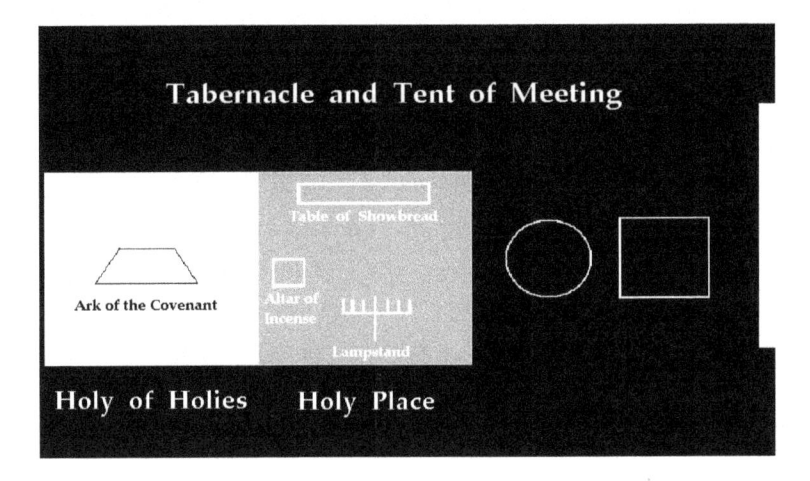

(Figure #3 – Layout of the Tent of Meeting)

The Holy of Holies had only one item in it and that was the Ark of the Covenant. (Fig. #3) The Ark represented the very presence of God. It was here that Moses would go to speak with God and get directions from Him.

I've always loved the descriptions of that time, picturing Moses going into the Tent and being in the very presence of God. Exodus 33:11 says,

> "The Lord would speak to Moses face to face, as a man speaks with his friend. Then Moses would return to the camp, but his young aide Joshua, son of Nun, did not leave the tent." (NIV)

I picture myself like Joshua, loving the presence of the Lord so much that even after Moses, his leader and friend had left, he would stay just to hang out in God's presence. It mirrors for me the account in the New Testament where two sisters, Martha and Mary, hosted a visit by Jesus. Martha, the eldest, was busy running around taking care of everyone, while Mary her younger sister, just wanted to be in Jesus' presence and hang out with Him. Do you know the Lord's presence? Do you know what it is to be refreshed by Him and hear from Him? It can only happen if you sit long enough in one place and desire to do so. He *will* speak to you and you *can* sense His presence. It's a privilege you have as one of His children.

As I have pointed out, the Tabernacle went where the Israelites went. When God said "move" it was packed up and carried to the next encampment where it was unfolded and set up again. That means it had to be flexible and portable.

My wife is fond of saying, when God told her to marry me she should "incorporate a sense of humor." (Good thing I'm a semi-secure person.) She also says that when we knew it was time to have children, God told her to "be flexible." Flexibility is a good thing. That means when the Tabernacle was set up it could adjust to the terrain and the surroundings on which it was to be placed. It's interesting how our prayer lives are affected by our surroundings! We should be willing to go wherever God sends us and be flexible enough to allow our prayer lives to be as vibrant as in the comfort of our homes.

I don't know if you are anything like me, but I like a place of familiarity when I pray, particularly when I'm alone. When we were first married, my wife and I lived in a trailer. It was not what I was used to. When we were single we were used to praying alone and out loud. We were both surprised to find out how uncomfortable we were to pray with someone in the next room. We didn't understand the need to be flexible and how our surroundings and life circumstances did affect our prayer lives.

There are two things I want you to understand about the Tabernacle. First, God made the way for His people to be with Him and effectively communicate with Him. Second, He had a purpose for each item inside the Tabernacle. With this in mind we can use the Tabernacle as a model for our daily walk with God and live out a healthy effective Christian life.

Chapter 5: Key #1 A Grateful Heart

Intro

Do you remember planning for and going on a trip you really felt you needed? It could have been something to either refresh you, like a vacation, or perhaps a business trip that would truly have far reaching effects. The excitement became your motivation for getting started, and making sure you got everything that you needed to begin. My wife Patti is our family's personal travel agent. She sends away for all the brochures about the area we will be visiting. She looks for sites to see, hotels to stay at, and cars to rent. She spends hours on the phone collecting information and making travel arrangements. She is a one-woman dynamo, even making back-up arrangements just in case we have problems with our initial choices.

Often, if you don't start right it makes everything else you do afterward that much harder, and you're not at ease. Our perspective is off when we don't have a good handle on what is going on. Perhaps we start in a panic, or in some desperate mode, reacting instead of being proactive. Preparing to pray is a lot like that I believe. We are often desperate and in need of something. Sometimes terrible things happen and we need comfort, so we jump into prayer without realizing our destination has a surer more direct path.

The ministry to the poor in our church, for example, delivers food to homes rather than having the needy come to our building. It gives us a chance, not only to touch those who are hungry, but also to meet with them in their surroundings, getting to know them, and ministering to them in many other areas of their lives. I make it a point to go out at least every second Friday, and there are often new people to deliver to. One of my delivery partners, who is female, would always make sure she mapped out the order in which we would make the deliveries. She had a baby so she couldn't come out with us for a time. I quickly learned the value of her example in planning ahead and starting out correctly. I, being a man, had no use for directions. I found myself wandering around the city for hours trying to find new locations. After I was thoroughly frustrated, I made sure we had a map and I knew where we were going and when. We needed to start right so that we could end right. This made our experience rewarding, fun, and effective.

Just Living Life

As we look at the Tabernacle and the First Key to a prosperous soul, we must realize that the priest, who ministered at the Tabernacle, was just like everyone else. He was just living life as they encamped around the Tabernacle. I see them fixing the tents they lived in, trying to resolve conflicts with their neighbors, raising their children, and all the other things associated with living life in a community. It couldn't have been easy for them. Each had their job to do, and they had to deal with life "on the road." Could you imagine living in such close proximity to your neighbors with nothing more than a couple of tent flaps separating you? Wow, no privacy there!

They were just living life in a community whose focus was the Lord. We, as the priests of God, are not immune from all the mundane and sometimes tedious duties associated with everyday life. And if you've been in the church for any length of time, you know that sometimes you feel like your business is everyone else's business. That can be good and that can be bad. It's good to know and be known, especially in the community of believers, but sometimes it comes with a price. Jesus never told us to hold up in a cave somewhere until He comes back. Rather we are to live with one another in love, working out "our issues" in faith, and "…whatever is true, whatever is noble, whatever is right, whatever is pure, whatever is lovely, whatever is admirable—if anything is excellent or praiseworthy—think about such things." (Phil. 4:8) (NIV) Not easy to do.

The Lord knows we are just trying to live life. We who know Him, and are filled with His Holy Spirit, are not exempt from the trials that come with living on earth. If you haven't noticed it is filled with others who don't see things the way you do. It's not easy for us. People hurt us and fail to meet our expectations. We get disappointed, our children don't always do what we want, our boss is not always very kind, and no matter how cautious we are, those driving on the same roads we on, don't always obey the rules. Yet, in this context we must start our journey into God's presence and pray with some kind of effectiveness.

The Way In

A psalmist gives us our First Key when he says in Psalm 100 (NIV),

> "Shout for joy to the Lord, all the earth. Worship the Lord with gladness; come before him with joyful songs. Know that the Lord is God. It is He who made us, and we are His; we are His people, the sheep of His pasture. *Enter His gates with thanksgiving and his courts with praise;* give thanks to Him and praise His name. For the Lord is good and His love endures forever; His faithfulness continues through all generations." (Emphasis mine)

We are to "Enter His gates with thanksgiving and His courts with praise." Gratitude is essential to having a healthy perspective of life, and the way we are to begin our journey into God's presence.

As a songwriter and worship leader, I can relate to the full expression of emotions that we see in the Psalms.

The writers don't hold back their feelings at all. They fully express their anger, frustrations, or feelings of abandonment, all in the midst of a "worship song." Because of their relationship with God, and being secure in it, they knew it was okay to express themselves. With this in mind they also knew, as this psalmist did, that the right perspective in approaching God is by giving thanks, and praising Him. Trying to enter any other way is illegal entry. It's like trying to break or sneak in.

As a boy growing up around sports, I loved to go to the football games of the local university. Because we didn't have money for such things, we would go up to the stadium and try any way we could to get in. We knew every hole in the fence, every nuance of ticket taking and how to slip through undetected. We would put on the little boy sad faces and ask those arriving on buses for extra tickets. That doesn't work with God, but I know some think it does.

How often do you find yourself needing to pray about something, but you start by complaining or immediately just start asking for things? In my estimation, that is illegal entry. Remember, God knows you and knows what you are going to pray before you even say or request it. (Matt. 6:8) With God as our Father, He provides for us, and has given us everything we need. We are to come before Him with grateful hearts.

As a father of two boys, how awesome it is when I hear them being grateful for the things provided for them. It shows respect, and it shows the right perspective of the overall picture of things. Their gratitude shows an understanding of how my wife and I have tried to provide what we feel they need most. When they have come to us complaining about what they lack, or just seem to want things without some recognition of the things they have already, our hearts drop, and unfortunately, I find myself less willing to give them what they desire. Thankfully our Father in heaven is not like me. He is ultimately patient and exceedingly kind.   He is all merciful and full of grace. Remember, grace is receiving something you don't deserve, and our Father in heaven is very gracious. Still, if we are to be ones who pray effectually we must come with hearts full of thanksgiving.

The Apostle Paul picks up this theme when he writes in Philippians 4:6 (NIV),

> "Do not be anxious about anything, but in everything, by prayer and petition, *with thanksgiving*, present your requests to God." (Emphasis mine)

He is trying to communicate that we all have anxious times, but why go there. We have one who can effect what we need affected. The way we do this is by prayer. Petitioning God for the things we need. However we don't come demanding or complaining about our lack, we come thankfully. We come as ones who know He has provided for us already, even giving us a means to get over our present anxiety. He has made the way and is the supplier of every need. He has not, and will not ever, let us down by refusing to give us what we need. How do I know this? God has already proven Himself by not holding back everything most precious to Him, and that is His one and only Son.

As a Pastor, I have seen people act in ways that they are later embarrassed about, specifically as believers in Jesus.

How selfish we can be. At times some will complain about the Lord not doing for them what they expect, and they get quite frustrated about it. In hearing this, I get a little frustrated myself, not at the Lord of course, but the one doing the complaining. It is at those times that I find myself saying, "What do you want Him to do? Die?" That's how far He has gone for us, and that's the perspective that must be realized. Give thanks to Him and praise Him for all He is and has done, because He has done a lot.

The word that is used for "thanksgiving" in Psalm 100 is "towdah," and it means to extend the hands, to avow, or confess something. The word for "praise" is "tehillah," which is to boisterously celebrate. The picture given in the use of these words is of a person looking toward heaven, proclaiming all God has done as an offering of worship. Psalm 92:1-6 (GW) says,

> "It is good to give thanks to the Lord, to make music to praise your name, O Most High. [2] It is good to announce your mercy in the morning and your faithfulness in the evening [3] on a ten-stringed instrument and a harp and with a melody on a lyre. [4] You made me find joy in what you have done, O Lord. I will sing joyfully about the works of your hands. [5] How spectacular are your works, O Lord! How very deep are your thoughts! [6] A stupid person cannot know and a fool cannot understand."

When we give thanks and praise to God, we are proving by our actions that the Lord is kind, and has been kind to us. He is faithful to us, even when we are faithless, as Paul says in 2 Timothy 2:13.

Often I will have our congregation stand and give thanks to the Lord, especially on Father's Day. It's a great time to offer up thanksgiving and praise for all God has done for us as our Father. In those times of corporate thanksgiving, we can all sense the blessing and immediate presence of the Lord. Psalm 22:3 (KJV) says God "inhabits the praises of Israel [His people]", therefore we can sense His presence, and we are enveloped by His glory.

So enter by giving Him thanks and praising His name. It is important how you start, and Key to having your soul prosper so that you can pray prayers that actually have effect.

So let's do it!

Take a moment and give this first Key a try. Here is a sample of how you might start:

"Lord I thank you for all you have done in my life. Thank you for rescuing me and showing me your great love. You are worthy to be praised, honored and glorified. No one compares to you and nothing is greater than you. All the good things in my life have come from you, so I thank you for them with all my heart." I thank you for…(fill in the blank)

It's your turn. Write a simple prayer of thanksgiving and praise here and pray it with all your heart. Remember your using the Tabernacle as the model so picture yourself walking through the gate.

(Your journey has just begun)

Chapter 6: Key #2 Confession

Intro

It was dusty and dirty on the road the Israelites traveled as they headed toward the Promised Land, and the priests got dirty just like everyone else. The dirt that collected on their bodies represented something. It symbolized the not-so-good things of this world that sticks to us, and if left unattended, causes our health to be affected. I can hear our parents now, "Did you wash your entire body...How about behind your ears?" I have two boys, and I get flashbacks every time they take a bath, or now...showers. "Joshua! Jonathan! Did you use a washcloth?" "I still see smudges on your face." Nag, nag, nag! I know what they're thinking as well, "Oh dad, I've already done that." They may even be thinking, "no one's going to see that, what's the big deal?" I see it, and they may not at first realize it, but so will everyone else...eventually.

Our next Key has this in mind. There was a "ceremonial washing" the Hebrew priest was to attend to before he went to worship God. God was showing them that they must wash off the things of this world that have affected them, whether they realized it or not. A basin filled with water, called the Laver, was placed between the Tent of Meeting and the Altar of Sacrifice (Fig. #1), and it was the first stop in their progression after entering the Tabernacle. The passage of scripture we are to apply here is 1 John 1:9 (NKJV),

> "If we confess our sins, he is faithful and just and will forgive us our sins and cleanse us from all unrighteousness."

Why would we need to be cleansed or purified from unrighteousness since we are already "positional-ly" righteous and clean through Jesus' death on the Cross? Obviously, we need it because our experiences, even as followers of Jesus, do not reflect our position.

The Laver and God's Unlimited Mercy

As I have mentioned, the Laver was the only structure within the Tabernacle that had no measurement. The Lord instructed Moses in Exodus 30:18–21 (NIV):

> "...Make a bronze basin, with its bronze stand, for washing. Place it between the Tent of Meeting and the altar, and put water in it. [19] Aaron and his sons are to wash their hands and feet with water from it. [20] Whenever they enter the Tent of Meeting, they shall wash with water so that they will not die. Also,

> when they approach the altar to minister by presenting an offering made to the Lord by fire, [21] they shall wash their hands and feet so that they will not die. This is to be a lasting ordinance for Aaron and his descendants for the generations to come."

As the Lord's disciples, we are of the priestly class, descendants of Aaron, and part of the "generations" Moses spoke of.

The Laver was made so that one could wash their hands and feet. Such symbolism cannot go unnoticed. To ceremonially wash ones hands was to declare innocence. Pilate washed his hands when condemning Jesus to death, ceremonially declaring his innocence in the shedding of Jesus' blood. David declared in Psalm 24:3–4 (NIV):

> "Who may ascend the hill of the Lord? Who may stand in his holy place? [4] He who has *clean hands* and a pure heart, who does not lift up his soul to an idol or swear by what is false." (Emphasis Mine)

So, who may ascend the hill of the Lord? Who may come into His presence, and stand in the Tabernacle's Holy Place? Who? He who has clean hands, in other words; he whose hands are innocent in the things they are applied to…the things *we* do. And since they were to wash their hands and feet, it also represented the places they have gone, their walk, if you will. Have you been places you shouldn't be? Is your walk with Christ as it should be? What have you put your hands to? Have you found yourself joining in on things you shouldn't have?

The Laver was to represent more than just a mere cleansing from the dirt of life, and we see this in the way it was made. It says in Exodus 38:8 (NIV):

> "They made the bronze basin and its bronze stand from the mirrors of the women who served at the entrance to the Tent of Meeting."

Who were these women and what were they doing at the entrance to the place of God's presence? We get a hint of who they were in subsequent passages in the Bible. Firstly, the word "served" in the NIV is also translated as "assembling" in the KJV. It is the Hebrew word "tsaba," which *is not* the word mostly used to describe the normal worship and ministry within the Tabernacle. That word is "sharath," and simply means to minister, attend, or serve, in the menial duties associated with worship inside the Tabernacle. The word "tsaba" is mostly used to describe assembling as to war, a mustering of troops in array for battle. It is a serious word, describing serious situations and people. Isaiah uses it to describe the Lord coming to do "battle" or "fight" for Mount Zion in the face of opposition. (Isaiah 31:4) So these women were "assembling" as serious people for God, in the face of personal opposition. In Luke 2:36–37 (NIV), we get a hint of who they were, and what they did;

> "There was also a prophetess, Anna, the daughter of Phanuel, of the tribe of Asher. She was very old; she had lived with her husband seven years after her marriage, and then was a widow until she was eighty-four. She never left the temple but worshiped night and day, fasting and praying."

This is the woman who prophesied over Jesus when Joseph and Mary brought Him to the Temple to be presented to the Lord. Anna was a serious woman who obviously found opposition in her life because she was only married for a short time. The implication here, in giving her age, is that she lost her husband when she was young, and therefore had been at the Temple a long time. She was a prophetess, no ordinary servant, who heard from God and spoke for Him. She served by fasting and praying, night and day. It was from women like Anna that Moses collected mirrors to be used to construct the Laver.

Isn't it interesting that highly polished bronze would be used? God has a purpose in everything, and for we who are serious about our relationship with the Lord, and about praying with impact, we must understand why this highly polished bronze…these "mirrors" were used. We cannot escape the obvious, and that is, mirrors are meant to reflect an image. Of course, they are mainly used to make sure we look all right, and for the women that used them it was no different. The funny thing about mirrors is that they don't lie. What you see is what you get. Yes…today is a bad hair day. How do I know? My mirror tells me so! To go around lauding a great hairdo when you, and everyone else knows it's not true, is plain dumb. A wise person would just admit it and humbly fix it.

When the priests would go to wash in the Laver, they could actually see themselves. It was a time of reflection. Was it just a reflection of outward appearances? Of course not! It was to be a reflection of who they were as followers of the One True God, and how they represented Him as priests.

For them, the Law of the Lord, handed down to them from Moses, was their benchmark. For us, it is a person...Jesus, who embodied the Law. He is the "Word" of God (John 1:1), and He has become our model for living. As the embodied "Word of God," He taught and spoke to us about the heart of the Law, and His words are life to us. Hebrews 7:28 (NIV) says:

> "For the law appoints as high priests men who are weak; but the oath, which came after the law, appointed the Son, who has been made perfect forever."

And in Hebrews 10:1(NIV) it says:

> "The law is only a shadow of the good things that are coming--not the realities themselves. For this reason it can never, by the same sacrifices repeated endlessly year after year, make perfect those who draw near to worship."

Also James 1:23–25(NIV) points out:

> "Anyone who listens to the word but does not do what it says is like a man who looks at his face in a mirror [24] and, after looking at himself, goes away and immediately forgets what he looks like. But the man who looks intently into the perfect law that gives freedom, and continues to do this, not forgetting what he has heard, but doing it—he will be blessed in what he does."

Jesus is the perfect man, reflecting the perfect law, and because of this we are being transformed into His likeness. Romans 8:29(NIV) says it best:

> "For those God foreknew he also predestined to be conformed to the likeness of his Son, that he might be the firstborn among many brothers."

We are being conformed into the likeness of Jesus, and when we look at Him and what He has taught us, it is as a reflection to us. How do you know your own image, what you look like? You look into a mirror. When we come to the Laver, on our way to prayer, we must look and see whose image we see. Is it the image and likeness of Jesus? If not, what part of what we see is contrary to Him? How do we know what Jesus looks like? His Word tells us. The Bible not only tells us what Jesus said, but what He did and how He did it. He truly is our standard and model for living.

Confessing Sins

We apply what we know about ourselves in reflecting Jesus through confession. Again, 1 John 1:9 starts, "*If* you confess your sins..." There is a condition placed on forgiveness, and that is confession. What are we confessing? We confess our sins. To sin means, "to miss the mark," as in a bulls-eye, and therefore not receive the prize. What mark, what bulls-eye are we aiming to hit? It is the image and likeness of Jesus.

The literal translation of the word "confess" is "to say the same word," or "to say the same thing." To say the same thing as who? To say the same thing as God is saying. If God says, 'that thing that you did [or said] is not right, that doesn't reflect me, you have sinned', we say…'that thing that I did or said is not right, that doesn't reflect you, I have sinned." We are agreeing with Him, and recognizing His Lordship over our lives. When we do this act of humility before God, we obtain something we don't deserve or merit in ourselves, and that is complete and unconditional forgiveness.

David, God's anointed ruler of His people Israel, was a man who knew how to sin. He could sin with the best of them, but he also was a man who knew how to repent and obey God. That is why he is called a "man after [God's] own heart." (1 Samuel 13:14) David had committed adultery with the wife of one of his soldiers, and then tried to cover it up when she was found to be pregnant. When this didn't work he had the man put in a position during a battle where he would be killed. After a time, Nathan the prophet came to David, and speaking for God, told David what he did, and how he sinned against God. David gives us an awesome example of confessing in Psalm 51 (NIV):

> "Have mercy on me, O God, according to your unfailing love; according to your great compassion blot out my transgressions. [2] Wash away all my iniquity and cleanse me from my sin. [3] For I know my transgressions, and my sin is always before me. [4] Against you, you only, have I sinned and done what is evil in your sight, so that you are proved right when you speak and justified when you judge. [5] Surely I was sinful at birth, sinful from the time my mother conceived me. [6] Surely you desire truth in the inner parts; you teach me wisdom in the inmost place. [7] Cleanse me with hyssop, and I will be clean; wash me, and I will be whiter than snow. [8] Let me

> hear joy and gladness; let the bones you have crushed rejoice. [9] Hide your face from my sins and blot out all my iniquity. [10] Create in me a pure heart, O God, and renew a steadfast spirit within me. [11] Do not cast me from your presence or take your Holy Spirit from me."

We see David hitting on everything 1 John 1:9 tells us, and how we need to approach God. He recognized it was against God that he sinned by missing the mark God had set up as the target. David knew he needed to be cleansed, washed with the water of forgiveness that only God could provide through His unlimited mercy. He also knew that it was a heart issue, not simply an issue of the act itself, so he prays that God would "create" or change his heart. God is the only one who can do that, and it's a heart change that we all need to reflect Him. Lastly, David knew that he wanted to be in God's presence, and that his sin had separated him from the very one he most desired to be with.

Applying, not begging for Forgiveness

Have you ever received a gift that you forgot you had? I believe anyone who has had a large wedding shower, and wedding, with all the gifts and things that come along with it, has gone out and purchased something they already owned but forgot about. I think of forgiveness like this. Jesus died on the Cross for ALL of our sins, not just the ones we remember. It's not a matter of asking Him to forgive us, He's already done that. It is a matter of applying what we already possess, we must take what He has given to us as a gift and put it to use. Remember, the Laver was the only thing in the Tabernacle that had no measure. Jesus' death is all that is needed, and the Cross, if you will, is like that Laver. There is no measurement for what Jesus did. We sing a song called "At The Cross," and it says, "At the Cross, You died for my sins, at the Cross you gave us life again." The Cross gives us new life…it makes us innocent before God all over again. When we look to what Jesus has accomplished on it we are healed, set free, and delivered. I love how Jesus said in John 3:14 (NIV):

> "Just as Moses lifted up the snake in the desert, so the Son of Man must be lifted up…"

The point is, God had Moses fashion a snake and lift it up on a pole so that when one of the Hebrews was bitten by a snake, if s/he would go and look at the snake, they would be healed and not die. Have you been bitten by a snake lately? Not a literal one, or a literal bite, but one like the serpent in the garden, who caused Adam and Eve to sin. If so, you need to run to the Cross, and to the one who hung on it. When you look at it, and the provisions there, you are healed, forgiven and set free from the things that separate you from God's presence.

Confession is all that is required. It is recognition of His Lordship in your life. Therefore when He says 'you have sinned', simply agree and say, 'I have sinned.' Also agree that Christ's sacrifice on the Cross is enough, and it is not a matter of begging Him for forgiveness, but applying that which He has provided on it. We are forgiven when we agree with God that we have fallen short, and that Christ's death is our means to being cleansed and made whole again.

Jesus destroyed the power of sin at the Cross, don't let the serpent convince you that somehow, this time, you've gone too far. When you sin and get dirty be like a little child…just jump in the tub and enjoy a good bath…the one your Father has prepared for you at the Laver.

Putting it together
Keys to a prospering soul are to:

1st Thanksgiving (Enter His Gates)

2nd Confession (Going to the Laver)

So let's do it!

Take a moment and give this second Key a try. Here is a sample of how you might start:

"Lord I am so sorry for all the things I do that do not reflect Jesus. Reveal to me now those things that I have done that offend you. I confess to you that I have_____, _____, and _____. I receive your forgiveness for all these things and I know that you wash me clean."

It's your turn. This time you'll be walking to the Laver to get clean. Write your confession on the next page:

Chapter 7: Key #3   Reconciliation

Intro

Here is a true account of reconciliation:

"Shortly after the turn of the century, Japan invaded, conquered, and occupied Korea. Of all of their oppressors, Japan was the most ruthless. They overwhelmed the Koreans with a brutality that would sicken the strongest of stomachs. Their crimes against women and children were inhuman. Many Koreans live today with the physical and emotional scars from the Japanese occupation. One group singled out for concentrated oppression was the Christians. When the Japanese army overpowered Korea one of the first things they did was board up the evangelical churches and eject most foreign missionaries. It has always fascinated me how people fail to learn from history. Conquering nations have consistently felt that shutting up churches would shut down Christianity. It didn't work in Rome when the church was established, and it hasn't worked since. Yet somehow the

Japanese thought they would have a different success record. The conquerors started by refusing to allow churches to meet, and jailing many of the key Christian spokesmen. The oppression intensified as the Japanese military increased its profile in the South Pacific. The "Land of the Rising Sum" spread its influence through a reign of savage brutality. Anguish filled the hearts of the oppressed and kindled hatred deep in their souls. One pastor persistently entreated his local Japanese police chief for permission to meet for services. His nagging was finally accommodated, and the police chief offered to unlock his church for one meeting. It didn't take long for word to travel. Committed Christians starving for an opportunity for unhindered worship quickly made their plans. Long before dawn on that promised Sunday, Korean families throughout a wide area made their way to the church. They passed the staring eyes of their Japanese captors, but nothing was going to steal their joy. As they closed the doors behind them, they shut out the cares of oppression and shut in a burning spirit anxious to glorify their Lord.

The Korean church has always had a reputation as a singing church. Their voices of praise could not be concealed inside the little wooden frame sanctuary. Song after song rang through the open windows into the bright Sunday morning. For a handful of peasants listening nearby, the last two songs this congregation sang seemed suspended in time. It was during a stanza of "Nearer My God to Thee" that the Japanese police chief waiting outside gave the orders. The people toward the back of the church could hear them when they barricaded the doors, but no one realized that they had doused the church with kerosene until they smelled the smoke. The dried wooden skin of the small church quickly ignited. Fumes filled the structure as tongues of flame began to lick the baseboard on the interior walls. There was an immediate rush for the windows. But momentary hope recoiled in horror as the men climbing out the windows came crashing back in, their bodies ripped by a hail of bullets. The good pastor knew it was the end. With a calm that comes from confidence, he led his congregation in a hymn whose words served as a fitting farewell to earth and a loving salutation to heaven. The first few words were all the prompting the terrified worshipers needed. With smoke burning their eyes, they instantly joined as one to sing their hope and leave their legacy. Their song became a serenade to the horrified and helpless witnesses outside. Their words also tugged at the hearts of the cruel men who oversaw this flaming execution of the innocent:

'Alas! and did my Savior bleed?
and did my Sovereign die?
Would he devote that sacred head
for such a worm as I?

Just before the roof collapsed they sang the last verse, their words an eternal testimony to their faith:

But drops of grief can ne'er repay
the debt of love I owe:
Here, Lord, I give myself away

'Tis all that I can do!
At the cross, at the cross
Where I first saw the light,
And the burden of my heart rolled away –
It was there by faith I received my sight,
And now I am happy all the day.'

The strains of music and wails of children were lost in a roar of flames. The elements that once formed bone and flesh mixed with the smoke and dissipated into the air. The bodies that once housed life fused with the charred rubble of a building that once housed a church. But the souls who left singing finished their chorus in the throne room of God. Clearing the incinerated remains was the easy part. Erasing the hate would take decades. For some of the relatives of the victims, this carnage was too much. Evil had stooped to a new low, and there seemed to be no way to curb their bitter loathing of the Japanese.

In the decades that followed, that bitterness was passed on to a new generation. The Japanese, although conquered, remained a hated enemy. The monument the Koreans built at the location of the fire not only memorialized the people who died, but stood as a mute reminder of their pain. Inner rest? How could rest coexist with bitterness deep as marrow in the bones? Suffering, of course, is a part of life. People hurt people. Almost all of us have experienced it at some time. Maybe you felt it when you came home to find that your spouse had abandoned you, or when your integrity was destroyed by a series of well-timed lies, or when your company was bled dry by a partner. It kills you inside. Bitterness clamps down on your soul like iron shackles.

The Korean people who found it too hard to forgive could not enjoy the "peace that passes all understanding." Hatred choked their joy.

It wasn't until 1972, that any hope came. A group of Japanese pastors traveling through Korea came upon the memorial. When they read the details of the tragedy and the names of the spiritual brothers and sisters who had perished, they were overcome with shame. Their country had sinned, and even though none of them were personally involved (some were not even born at the time of the tragedy), they still felt a national guilt that could not be excused. They returned to Japan committed to right a wrong. There was an immediate outpouring of love from their fellow believers. They raised ten million yen ($25,000). The money was transferred through proper channels and a beautiful white church building was erected on the sight of the tragedy. When the dedication service for the new building was held, a delegation from Japan joined the relatives and special guests.

Although their generosity was acknowledged and their attempts at making peace appreciated, the memories were still there. Hatred preserves pain. It keeps the wounds open and the hurts fresh. The Koreans' bitterness had festered for decades. Christian brothers or not, these Japanese were descendants of a ruthless enemy. The speeches were made, the details of the tragedy recalled, and the names of the dead honored. It was time to bring the service to a close. Someone in charge of the agenda thought it would be appropriate to conclude with the same two songs that were sung the day the church was burned. The song leader began the words to "Nearer My God to Thee." But something remarkable happened as the voices mingled on the familiar melody. As the memories of the past mixed with the truth of the song, resistance started to melt. The inspiration that gave hope to a doomed collection of churchgoers in a past generation gave hope once more. The song leader closed the service with the hymn "At the Cross." The normally stoic Japanese could not contain themselves. The tears that began to fill their eyes during the song suddenly gushed from deep inside. They turned to their Korean spiritual relatives and begged them to forgive. The guarded, calloused hearts of the Koreans were not quick to surrender. But the love of the Japanese believers, not intimidated by decades of hatred, tore at the Koreans' emotions.

'At the cross, at the cross
Where I first saw the light,
And the burden of my heart rolled away ...'

One Korean turned toward a Japanese brother. Then another. And then the floodgates holding back a wave of emotion let go. The Koreans met their new Japanese friends in the middle. They clung to each other and wept. Japanese tears of repentance and Korean tears of forgiveness intermingled to bathe the site of an old nightmare. Heaven had sent the gift of reconciliation to a little white church in Korea." (Tim Kimmel, *Little House on the Freeway,* pp. 56–61.)[1]"

One of the least practiced spiritual exercises in the church today is Reconciliation. As Christian people, we should be showing the world what it is and how to do it, but if we were to truly be honest, we'd have to admit we have not been very good at it. It is sad to think that some of the worst break-ups, misunderstandings, and displays of stubbornness I have seen, have occurred between people within the Church of Jesus Christ. When unleashed, reconciliation becomes a powerful component in our arsenal against those things that try to hinder our prayers, and wreck our souls.

Jesus recognized the relationship between our ability to surrender our lives completely to God, and our interpersonal relationships. There is a direct correlation between how we treat others, and our ability to fully experience all of what God has for us. My wife and I have always said that there is nothing in this world that will make you grow into the likeness of Christ then marriage. Those of us who are married know what I am talking about. If you want to get along, you've got to be attentive to another's feelings and concerns, or it will affect you…sooner or later. That is true for all of us however, whether we're married or not. We do not live life in a fish bowl. What we do affects others, and what others do effects us. Jesus had this in mind when He said in Matthew 5:23–24 (NIV):

> "Therefore, if you are offering your gift at the altar and there remember that your brother has something against you, [24] leave your gift there in front of the

altar. First go and be reconciled to your brother; then come and offer your gift."

The next Key in our progression through the Tabernacle for the purposes of effective praying is Reconciliation. After the Priests came into the Tabernacle to worship, they would go to the Laver, and then head for the Altar to make a sacrifice. This is the Altar Jesus is referring to when He tells His listeners, 'Hey! Don't bother offering God any gifts of sacrifice when you know there is something between you and your brother." Why would He say that? Do you think He considered our interpersonal relationships to have effect upon our freedom to obey Him and do what He requires? There is no doubt that He did. When I look at my own life and my walk with the Lord, it is obvious that I can see a hindrance to the work of the Lord in my life when I am not "right" with those closest to me.

Who is my brother?

We must ask then, as others have, 'Who is my brother'? The word is used to describe natural family and literal brothers, as well as those who are of the family of God. Jesus told the disciples in Mathew 23:8(NIV):

> "But you are not to be called 'Rabbi,' for you have only one Master and *you are all brothers.*"(Emphasis mine)

We are all brothers, each of us who are called by the Name of Jesus, and therefore we are not to have anything between us.

That's heavy…isn't it? Well, it's not supposed to be, because as the song says, "He ain't heavy, he's my brother." Yet when we look at all that goes on around us, and the divisions within the Church, it does seen monumental, but that's a topic for another time. We will deal with our personal relationships, and how we can work out this call of Christ to "be Reconciled" to our brothers so that we can complete our course through God's Tabernacle, and into His presence to pray with impact.

> Let's look at our verse of scripture again:
>
> "Therefore, if you are offering your gift at the altar and there remember that your brother has something against you, leave your gift there in front of the altar. First go and be reconciled to your brother; then come and offer your gift."

I love how Jesus covers all the bases. He doesn't want us to be bound by anything or anyone. He didn't say 'that you have something against your brother,' He said you "remember that your brother has something against you." We'll be talking about the former in a couple of chapters.

I misread this verse for years, but then came face to face with a situation in which I was forced to revisit God's instructions and saw my own bias. While an Assistant Pastor at a church my wife and I helped establish, we believed it was time for us to leave and seek the Lord for the future. After several months, and with the encouragement of our Overseer, we knew the Lord was calling us to "plant" a church. We knew it would be hard, but we wanted to be obedient to what we believed, and was later confirmed (in that it happened) to be God's will for us. We thought everything was fine between our former Pastor and us, but later came to realize he was not happy about our new direction.

If only I had known then what I know now about Reconciliation! I could have saved all of us months of discomfort, misunderstanding, and separation. I thought, stubbornly, that I didn't need to go to him because it was his problem, not mine. I wasn't holding anything against him. I had no un-forgiveness in my heart, so it would be up to him to just get over it…right?! Wrong! Jesus didn't say 'if you have something against your brother,' He said, "your brother has something against you." I was so humbled when at a national Pastors' gathering; my former Pastor came to me during one of the breaks and sought reconciliation. Immediately this scripture came to me, and it was as if the words were highlighted to me, "your brother has something against you!" I was so grateful for the opportunity for reconciliation with him. It was as if the cloud, which I had accepted as being part of my life, was lifted. What freedom! Where before my prayer life was constantly invaded by thoughts of a separated relationship, it was now free to focus on whatever God had for me to apply myself to. I later apologized to him, saying that I should have been the one to go to him but did not. We even got our two congregations together for a night of worship, prayer and reconciliation. What an awesome time, and what a great lesson.

The Greek word for Reconciliation has the idea of simply making the situation different. In other words, change it. For me, there was a separation between brothers-in-the-faith, and that does not represent God's will for His

Holy family. So, it became different through change, and that change we call Reconciliation.

As far as it is with you

In trying to live a life of Reconciliation with my brothers and sisters, one thing has become painfully apparent, not everyone is willing to go there. That's a sad commentary on our ever present ever encroaching fallen state, or as Paul puts it, our "sin nature." (Romans 7)

One of my personal/ministerial goals is to have as much relationship with as many Pastors as I can, especially with those in our geographic area. I believe to *truly* pastor people in any region, and to see the Kingdom of God expanded in that region Pastors must have relationship with one another. Especially in today's consumer oriented society in which people move around so freely. I'm so grateful that the Pastors of our area get together regularly for prayer and outreach activities. What a blessing to see Pastors of various traditions coming together. Catholics, Pentecostals, Evangelicals, Mainline, and Independent churches, all with the same heart, and that is, Jesus Christ and His Kingdom. Yet some still refuse to do so. I have friends of mine who are Pastors, who will get together with me and some others, but refuse to get together with each other because of some past difference. Isn't that sad? And if we're sad about it, how must Our Father in heaven feel?

Though this is the unfortunate case with some, it cannot be for you and me. Therefore, as far as it is with us, we must at least offer reconciliation. We find that some will accept, others will not. We are responsible for what we do before God, but we cannot force others to comply. If you have tried to reconcile with others and they have rejected your sincere advances, you can be assured you are right before God. Make sure, however, that no bitterness grows in you toward them. You must always be open to reconciling with others, even if the offer comes late. Here are some Proverbs that may help:

> Proverbs 17:17 "A friend loves at all times, and a brother is born for adversity."
>
> Proverbs 18:19 "An offended brother is more unyielding than a fortified city, and disputes are like the barred gates of a citadel."
>
> Proverbs 27:17 "As iron sharpens iron so one man sharpens another."
>
> Proverbs 17:9 "He who covers over an offense promotes love, but whoever repeats the matter separates close friends."
>
> Proverbs 19:11 "A man's wisdom gives him patience; it is to his glory to overlook an offense."

Therefore, be the wise and understanding one and apply what Jesus teaches. When you are going into the Lord's presence to pray, and you're headed for the Altar to make your sacrifice (you'll find out what that is), if He reminds you that one of His family has something against you, go and make it different between you. You won't regret it, for your soul will truly prosper!

Putting it together

Keys to a prospering soul are to:

1st Thanksgiving (Enter His Gates)

2nd Confession (Going to the Laver)

3rd Reconciliation (On the way to the Alter)

So let's do it!

Take a moment and give this third Key a try. Here is a sample of how you might start:

"Lord please give me the courage to be reconciled with _____. Prepare the way for us to make it different between us. If there is anyone else who you know is holding something against me as well, show me that I may also be reconciled with them."

It's your turn. Write down your heart's desire for reconciliation with those who hold something against you:

Chapter 8: Key #4 Surrender

Intro

Woody Allen once said, "It's not that I'm afraid to die, I just don't want to be there when it happens.[1]" This pretty much sums up many of our attitudes toward our next stop through the Tabernacle. If there is one thing we are called to do as Christ-followers, it is to die; die to ourselves, this world, and all that comes along with it. That's why Paul says in Galatians 2:20 (NIV):

> "I have been crucified with Christ and I no longer live, but Christ lives in me. The life I live in the body, I live by faith in the Son of God, who loved me and gave himself for me."

He saw himself as a living breathing dead man. As one crucified with Christ, he is stating that Jesus' sacrifice on the Cross literally killed the old Paul, nailing him there with Jesus, and resurrected a new Paul, who was now empowered by the Holy Spirit. Knowing that this act of surrender is for everyone, he urges us to lay down our lives each and every day, and refers to the Tabernacle to do so saying in Romans 12:1(NIV):

> "Therefore, I urge you, brothers, in view of God's mercy, to offer your bodies as living sacrifices, holy and pleasing to God—this is your spiritual act of worship."

The "act of worship" he is referring to is a sacrifice made at the altar of God either in the Tabernacle or the Temple. For we who now have the Living Lord inside of us, His sacrifice on the cross as the Lamb of God was once and for all, needing never to be repeated, this was not the case with the sacrifices of animals in the Tabernacle. Our "spiritual act of worship" is not our literal death, but the offering of ourselves to God in heart, mind and body. We have no life outside of Jesus. We are His instruments to be used as He pleases.

A Sacrifice is Suppose to be Dead

Easier said than done should be your first response to this Key. The one thing we don't do easily is die. Have you ever seen a really, really old movie, especially the silent films? They were great! I particularly enjoyed the death scenes when the actor would ham-up his final moments. They seemed to go on forever. With the back of one hand on their foreheads, looking up as they leaned on the other, in the final throe's of life, they were going to get as much on-screen time as possible.

Living here and now on planet earth, in the good ol' US of A, we are no different. We want to get as much out of life as we possibly can. That in and of itself is not a bad thing, but when it becomes an insatiable desire for self-gratification, we miss the point of true living, and in particular, living for Christ.

"Fifty-six men signed the Declaration of Independence. Their conviction resulted in untold sufferings for themselves and their families. Of the 56 men, five were captured by the British and tortured before they died. Twelve had their homes ransacked and burned. Two lost their sons in the Revolutionary Army. Another had two sons captured. Nine of the fifty-six fought and died from wounds or hardships of the war. Carter Braxton of Virginia, a wealthy planter and trader, saw his ships sunk by the British Navy. He sold his home and properties to pay his debts and died in poverty. At the battle of Yorktown, the British General Cornwallis had taken over Thomas Nelson's home for his headquarters. Nelson quietly ordered General George Washington to open fire on the Nelson home. The home was destroyed and Nelson died bankrupt. John Hart was driven from his wife's bedside as she was dying. Their thirteen children fled for their lives. His fields and mill were destroyed. For over a year, he lived in forests and caves, returning home only to find his wife dead and his children vanished. A few weeks later, he died from exhaustion.[2]"

When I think of the sacrifices made by those who stood up for what they believed, I am reminded of John Henry Jowett's words, "Ministry that costs nothing, accomplishes nothing." Sacrifices hurt. If it doesn't hurt, it probably isn't much of a sacrifice. King David, in his desire to obey God, refused the offer of Araunah, a simple farmer, to give David his threshing floor for free. David was to erect an Altar there for the Lord. He instead answered, "…No, I insist on paying the full price. I will not take for the Lord what is yours, or sacrifice a burnt offering that costs me nothing." (1 Chron. 21:24) (NIV) To truly obey God, and live for Him, which He is asking us to do, we must sacrifice that which means the most to us…our very lives. The Kingdom of God is the only thing indisputably worth giving our lives to, and we are then, dead to ourselves and to this world's promises.

Total Surrender

Let's look again at our scripture from Romans 12:

> "Therefore, I urge you, brothers, in view of God's mercy, to offer your bodies as living sacrifices, holy and pleasing to God--this is your spiritual act of worship."

Paul is pleading with us here because this is a big deal and this means something. He is not saying it because he needs to fill up his letter to the Roman church. He wants us to understand the practical applications of our salvation. The Romans were known to be very practical people, until they grew decadent beyond any sense of wisdom, and for such it is said that "Greeks have Philosophy, and Romans build roads." Paul, in a larger sense, was giving them the practical understanding of what it means to be a Christ-follower. It wasn't about some high-minded ideal, which has no earthly implications outside of its proliferators. No, it was about the very purpose of living life and how to live it to the full. He tells them to present, or to offer, their literal bodies. He wanted their physical beings to reflect what had happened to them spiritually. Even more than that, he wanted them to literally present themselves as an offering before God. God indeed is still looking for sacrifices, and it is the very bodies of His people. You've heard it said many times before, "God uses people." He uses people as instruments of His glory…His hands and feet if you will. In this sense, we are "living sacrifices." We totally surrender ourselves to His purposes through us each and every day.

The sacrifices offered in the Tabernacle were to be separated out for the purposes of God, perfect and without blemish, often the first-born of some species of animal, or the first-fruits of some produce. As such, they were Holy and pleasing to the Lord. Pleasing because they weren't supposed to be the leftovers or second or third best. It was the best, the first-fruits. Too often, I had found myself giving God my leftover time, energy and money, and I have come to realize that this is not the sacrifice He requires. I was giving Him the sacrifice of Cain, while I saw others being blessed and wondered why. (Genesis 4:1–7) This is not easy. It is definitely the narrow road Jesus speaks about in Matthew 7:13–14, and if we truly want to experience a prospering soul, and to see the Kingdom of God working through us, we can only enter through that "narrow gate."

Paul describes this sacrifice as our "act of worship," or as the KJV translates it, our "reasonable service." As a Worship Leader, I have a high value for heart-felt and sincere worship of God, and to see God's people expressing themselves in the context of a church service whether through the playing of instruments, singing or the like. The word most used for "worship" in the New Testament is "proskuneo," and it could be somewhat succinctly understood as turning toward God and showing Him affection. I like to see what we do in the midst of a worship set on Sundays as this very act of expressing ourselves to Him in intimate and revealing tunes. The word for worship that Paul is using in Romans 12:1, is not "proskuneo" however, but "latreia." It is one that is best translated service, and often accompanies the description of ministry in the Tabernacle (Hebrews 9:6). It was accomplished by the Priests of God as a physical undertaking of the ordinances of God. It is what He required. We often have too restricted a view of worship, relegating it simply to our participation in a Sunday morning or weekly praise time. We worship God every time we bow to His desires and commands. To me, each decision we make that sides with what God would have us do is worship. When we agree with God and His Word, and subsequently reject the enemies' enticements, we are worshipping God. In the context of Romans 12, Paul says that the offering of our bodies as living sacrifices is this "act of worship." It is the logical thing for us to do in the worship of God. It is the physical use of our bodies in the service of God in whatever capacity He desires, going where He wants us to go, doing what He wants us to do.

Therefore, when I'm praying through this Key, I say such things as, "Lord, I surrender my life to you today. This is Your day, use me as You will."

Putting it together

Keys to a prospering soul are to:

1st Thanksgiving (Enter His Gates)

2nd Confession (Going to the Laver)

3rd Reconciliation (On the way to the Altar)

4th Surrender (At the Altar)

So let's do it!

Take a moment and give this fourth Key a try. Here is a sample of how you might start:

"Lord I lay down my life before you today as a sacrifice. I have given my life to you so use me anyway you want to. My life is yours, my will is yours, my emotions are yours, and even that which I do as routine are all yours. Work through me today for your Kingdom's purposes"

It's your turn. Write your prayer of surrender here and pray it with all your heart:

Chapter 9: Key #5 Forgiveness

Intro

There is no Key more important to living a healthy life than recognizing the Power of Forgiveness. If more people knew how to practice the art of forgiveness, I truly believe the overwhelming need for Psychiatrists and Physiologist would be greatly diminished. Just imagine it, insurance premiums would be reduced, (that would be nice) road-rage would become non-existent, the days of family members not speaking to one another would vanish...all because they not only know about forgiveness, but actually practice it. I know...you think I'm dreaming or I'm just not in touch with reality. You and my "shrink" are the only ones...what do you all know! It would be nice though wouldn't it?

I'm sorry to say that even among believing people, un-forgiveness runs rampant, infecting themselves, their families, and those who have wronged them in some way. I would go as far as to say that we, as Christ-followers, are quite weak at practicing true forgiveness. Though we are the ones who should be modeling forgiveness to the world, we end up sadly being the ones looked upon as practicing the opposite. I believe this, not because we don't know we should, or that we don't make an attempt at it, but because we are ignorant of its true ramifications and simply how to do it. I especially find among Christians the disbelief that they haven't forgiven, because when I approach them about needing to forgive someone, they reply in a frustrated, red-faced tone, "I've already done that!" We know we are suppose to forgive, and we may even say we forgive someone because we don't want to look "unspiritual," either to our ourselves or to others, by admitting we still hold something against someone else. I often reply, 'if you truly have forgiven, how come every time their name is mentioned, or you think about them, you grit your teeth and your brow gets all wrinkly?' This is what this chapter is all about...ridding people of their wrinkly brows!

Someone once said, "Forgiveness is a lovely idea until you have something to forgive." Being wronged by someone is not easy, and outside the laboratory, it really hurts. We battle many things in the midst of being hurt by someone, especially if that person is close to us. Confusion, rejection, misunderstanding, and a host of other feelings flood over us as we try to swim against the current of our pain. Because of a lack of understanding we consider forgiveness an "event" rather than seeing it as it truly is, a "process."

In using the Tabernacle as our model to walk a renewed life daily, the next stop in our trek is back to the Laver before entering into the Holy Place and the Holy of Holies where God's presence resides. The priests who ministered in the Tabernacle would not only go to the Laver before making a sacrifice at the Altar, but also afterwards, specifically before they entered the "Tabernacle Proper," also known as the "Tent of Meeting." Again, it was symbolic of cleansing, and this time because nothing unholy can stand before the Lord, including our un-forgiveness.

Our main verse of scripture for this section comes from Mark 11:25 (NIV):

> "And when you stand praying, if you hold anything against anyone, forgive him, so that your Father in heaven may forgive you your sins."

Since we are describing a devotional prayer life, this verse becomes quite apropos, especially when we consider that within the Tabernacle, one of the main things we will be doing is praying, and as I have pointed out, we want our prayers to be effective and powerful. The one thing that will certainly weaken the prayers you pray is un-forgiveness. So let's look at this more closely, and learn the power that resides in forgiveness.

Un-forgiveness Equals Bondage

It is amazing how strong the language of the Bible is concerning forgiveness. Jesus says, specifically, 'if you don't forgive…you can't be forgiven.' (my paraphrase) Just look at our main verse for this section, "…forgive...so that your Father in heaven may forgive you…" There is a contingency placed upon our own forgiveness. Let's look at some other verses:

> Matthew 6:14–15 "For if you forgive men when they sin against you, your heavenly Father will also forgive you. [15] But if you do not forgive men their sins, your Father will not forgive your sins."

> Luke 6:37 "Do not judge, and you will not be judged. Do not condemn, and you will not be condemned. Forgive, and you will be forgiven."

> John 20:23 "If you forgive anyone his sins, they are forgiven; if you do not forgive them, they are not forgiven."

These are wonderful verses of scripture. They are given for us to understand the relationship between our own authority and accountability as Christ-followers, and the work accomplished for us at the Cross.

There is a revealing discourse in the Bible concerning this relationship and the subsequent manner people are directly affected and affected negatively, if not heeded. *Unforgiveness binds us up*. Let's look at it in its two major sections. First:

Matthew 18:15–22 (NIV) "If your brother sins against you, go and show him his fault, just between the two of you. If he listens to you, you have won your brother over. [16] But if he will not listen, take one or two others along, so that 'every matter may be established by the testimony of two or three witnesses.' [17] If he refuses to listen to them, tell it to the church; and if he refuses to listen even to the church, treat him as you would a pagan or a tax collector. [18] "I tell you the truth, *whatever you bind on earth will be bound in heaven, and whatever you loose on earth will be loosed in heaven.* [19]"Again, I tell you that if two of you on earth agree about anything you ask for, it will be done for you by my Father in heaven. [20] For where two or three come together in my name, there am I with them." [21] "Then Peter came to Jesus and asked, "Lord, how many times shall I forgive my brother when he sins against me? Up to seven times?" [22] Jesus answered, "I tell you, not seven times, but seventy-seven times [or seventy times seven]. (Bracketed addition mine)

What we need to recognize here is how others, or those we hold things against, are directly affected by our unforgiveness. In the context of this passage, starting with verse 15, the topic is "…your brother sins against you…" in other words; forgiveness is needed because someone has wronged you. Peter knew what Jesus was referring to because he asked the question in verse 21, "…how many times shall I forgive my brother…?"

The first question that begs to be asked again is 'who is my brother?' The word is "adelphos", and is used mainly to describe those closest to you, in other words "brethren". It can be your literal family, the family of God, or even kinsmen (ie. Paul considered all Israelites his brothers. [Romans 9:3]) I believe, however, to get hung up on such a thing as "who is my brother," in this context is like straining out a gnat and swallowing a camel. Really, forgiveness is for everyone...its "all men", as in Matthew 16:14–15. Thank God, Jesus' death on the Cross was for *all* mankind not just a particular people group. He gave us the ultimate example of forgiveness to all men, when he said while hanging on the Cross, "Father forgive them, they don't know what they are doing." Who? Who put him on the Cross? The Jews, the Romans? He was put there to die for *all* mankind, every one of us. Unfortunately, I have encountered those who tried to justify not forgiving someone because the people who hurt them were not Christians, or not "acting like a Christian." Unwittingly, with such a comment, they were proving the fact that those who refuse to forgive place themselves and others into bondage that needs to be broken.

Jesus said to the disciples, "...I tell you the truth, whatever you bind on earth will be bound in heaven, and whatever you loose on earth will be loosed in heaven." The word bind is "deo" and simply means to tie-up, whether it be an animal, so it won't run away, or a person to be your captive. So, when we hold people to account for their wrongs against us here on earth, we, in essence, are binding them in the spiritual realm of heaven as well. WE PUT THEM IN CHAINS! Think about it. Why is Jesus so tough against us if we don't forgive, even going as far as to say that our forgiveness is contingent upon our being able to forgive others? Again, it goes back to the Cross. He paid a heavy price for our sins, forgiving us for all of them. Not only that, as it says in Luke 4, He came to free captives, and those who are oppressed. In other words, un-forgiveness does the very opposite of what He came to herald, and we as His representatives are to model who He is, and what He came to do. God is so hard about the topic of forgiveness because when we show and practice it, we are truly representing Him. To hold people to account without giving them the means to repent is the antithesis of all He is about.

      How are people placed in chains? As far as their relationship is with you, they will never change. They may be able to overcome many areas in their own lives, but when it comes to how you see them, and your own relationship with them, they cannot. Why, because you are holding them in that place where they hurt you to account for their sins against you. In essence, you have chained them to that place/event to be identified with it until which time you release them from it. It's a prison of *your* making. You are the only one with the key. You are the warden; the jailer; the judge; the jury and you carry out the sentence. They are your captives, and as a Christ-follower, with the anointing that you possess, you have bound them spiritually to the dirty deed done. They are forever associated with it, as far as it is with you. Christ's mission was to reconcile men to His Father in heaven. In other words, make it different between us and God. Where we were once separate because of the sin of our forebears, now our relationship is healed by the blood of Jesus. Where we were in chains, unregenerate and unholy, because of this separation un-forgiven, we are now free because of right relationship with God through Jesus. Forgiveness is the beginning of the reconciliation process. First, God forgave us, then we accepted that forgiveness and were reconciled to Him. It is the same thing between you and whoever wrongs you. First you forgive, they are released from the chains associated with it, and then a difference can be made in your relationship with them. However, you can only do your part, you cannot dictate what someone else will do. It is a two-part process...you forgive, they accept. When you choose not to forgive, you, as well as they, are affected adversely.

This brings us to our second section in the passage concerning what happens when we don't forgive in Matthew 18:23-35 (NIV):

> [23] "Therefore, the kingdom of heaven is like a king who wanted to settle accounts with his servants. [24] As he began the settlement, a man who owed him ten thousand talents was brought to him. [25] Since he was not able to pay, the master ordered that he and his wife and his children and all that he had be sold to repay the debt. [26] "The servant fell on his knees before him. 'Be patient with me,' he begged, 'and I will pay back everything.' [27] The servant's master took pity on him, canceled the debt and let him go. [28] "But when that servant went out, he found one of his fellow servants who owed him a hundred denari. He grabbed him and began to choke him. 'Pay back what you owe me!' he demanded. [29] "His fellow servant fell to his knees and begged him, 'Be patient with me, and I will pay you back.' [30] "But he

refused. Instead, he went off and had the man thrown into prison until he could pay the debt. [31] When the other servants saw what had happened, they were greatly distressed and went and told their master everything that had happened. [32] "Then the master called the servant in. 'You wicked servant,' he said, 'I canceled all that debt of yours because you begged me to. [33] Shouldn't you have had mercy on your fellow servant just as I had on you?' [34] In anger his master turned him over to the jailers to be tortured, until he should pay back all he owed. [35] "This is how my heavenly Father will treat each of you unless you forgive your brother from your heart."

This awesome parable illustrates quite vividly what happens when forgiveness is not applied. The "king" here is one who forgave freely and generously. The "servant" chose to hold another to account, even after experiencing the gift of forgiveness given him by the king. God is our King, and He forgave us everything. We are His servants, and we are trying to do that which He has modeled to us. If we don't forgive, just as we have been forgiven, "from the heart," we are handed over to the jailers to be tortured. We put ourselves into bondage by our actions. We don't experience "The Rack" or "Thumbscrews" in our being tortured, but we do experience things in our emotions, and at times, in our physical bodies, which are tortuous. Things like anger, jealousy, bitterness, envy, rage, and sometimes high blood pressure, arthritis, and a host of other inflictions can occur. When we experience such things as bitterness, anger, envy etc., it is a sure sign that we are most likely holding something against someone. I tell people all the time… "This is not rocket science," though I believe rocket science is easier to apply. If you are feeling such things in your day, it is a sign to you, and you must ask the question 'who do I need to forgive?' If you ask that question, and don't really know, God will show you.

I cannot tell you how often we have ministered to someone with a physical ailment, and in the process of that ministry, found out that someone had wronged them. When they were able to release the person by speaking forgiveness to them right there and then, we could see the miracle of healing come where nothing else worked before. Just recently, there was a girl in our church; I'll call her Ruby, who came to us because she had a skin disease that no ointment or medication would heal. During a time of ministry at one of our groups, she was able to forgive someone from her past who had done unspeakable things to her. As a result her skin problem simply and immediately disappeared. I know she was happy...and we continue to thank God for what He has done for us at the Cross...freedom!

A model for forgiving

Have you ever observed someone doing some task or routine, and thought to yourself, 'I wish I could do that?' Maybe you've grabbed hold of a process for doing something that benefited you in ways you could not otherwise have done unless you had implemented that process. That's all a model is, and at times they fit us and at times they do not. I am one who doesn't like to talk about something and give no way of working it out in every day life. That's a primary drive, even for the writing of this book. It is from this point of view that I want to share with you a model for forgiving others that has benefited my wife and me ever since we were taught it many years ago. Where it actually originated we do not know, but one thing we do know is we practice it constantly. If it seems right to you, and it fits you, please do it and do it as often as needed.

Just like any good model, we have passed it on to as many as possible and we have seen those who have put it in to practice come back with wonderful testimonies of changed lives. One woman in particular comes to mind. She was one whose brother had done things to her as a little girl a brother should not do. Now as an adult, she was struggling in areas of her life, and she needed freedom from the torture that she was experiencing. She was married with children, yet her relationship with her brother was hanging over her head. Her brother, who lived in another country, had not spoken to her in years. She came to me and asked what she should do. I taught her the model I am about to show you, and the results were astounding. Because we believe forgiveness is a process and not just an event, and that those who are closest to us hurt us the deepest, therefore often taking longer to work out, I gave her some instructions. I told her that whenever she thought of her brother, if she could not do it without grimacing, she needed to practice the model, even if she had to do it every day for a year. She agreed, and just about one year later, she came to me very excited and told me her brother had called and wanted to come for a visit. She asked me what she should do, and I told her to say yes. After some days of visiting, her brother broke down crying in front of her, asking her to forgive him and wishing reconciliation...this happened without her even broaching the topic of his past sins against her! You see, he was bound and needed to be released, in particular loosed by his sister whom he had sinned against. When she did so, freedom came to their relationship, and she experienced healing in many other areas of her own life as well.

We call this model the "Five Step Healing Model,"...why?...because it contains five steps. You brainiac you! You knew that all along. Yes, I know that was unnecessary, I was just trying to insult you so you can have someone to practice on after you were done reading. By the way, these steps are to be done in a time of prayer by yourself or with someone you are ministering to, and not with the person who wronged you. Why? Because we have found that when we go to the person who wronged us, still with bitterness and un-forgiveness on our hearts, we are setting ourselves up for more frustration and anger. This is especially true if the person doesn't have any idea of what they have done, or is not mature enough to receive our overtures to healing. We often come away from such an encounter with more hurts and even more un-forgiveness to deal with.

Here is the model:

1. EMPTY THE GARBAGE CAN — We are like human garbage compactors... someone hurts us and we stuff it, someone else hurts us and we stuff that, and again someone else wrongs us in another way and we do the same. We do this until the time when our can gets so full that seemingly some very

small and insignificant event makes the whole thing spill over, and God help the person who happens to be there when it does. What a mess, and unfortunately, what a clean up is needed. The remedy? Empty the can when it has something in it. Even with small amounts of garbage, if left there long enough it starts to smell, and you don't want to smell bad do you? The way we do this is simple. At a time alone, preferably during a quite time with the Lord while walking through the Tabernacle, we will speak to the person who wronged us, just as if they were there, telling them all they have done to us. This may take two seconds or two hours, but whatever the case, we do it until we have gotten out that which we need to.

2. SPEAK OUT FORGIVENSS FROM THE HEART — Once we have spoken out the wrong(s) done to us, as best we can, from our hearts, we say something like, 'Even though you have done this to me, I forgive you.' This is only the second step however, and there's three more to go....hmmmm, I wonder why?

3. ASK THE LORD TO FORGIVE THE PERSON — Jesus, while hanging on the Cross, gave us a wonderful example of forgiveness when He said, "Father forgive them, they don't know what they are doing." (Luke 23:34) This is important for a couple of reasons: (a) It is a recognition of the relationship between myself and God, and truly whatever I bind on earth, will be bound in heaven. (b) It is like a test

step. I have found people who don't want God to forgive, they want Him to remember. 'Vengeance is yours Lord, vengeance is yours!' All of a sudden they are Old Testaments scholars. They may start quoting some of their favorite Psalms, which in a paraphrase may say something like, 'Rip their eyes out, oh God, … pull out their toe nails my Rock and my Redeemer,' something like that. Unfortunately, I don't believe that's what Jesus had in mind. What we are supposed to be doing is asking God to release them from the wrongs they have done to us, even though we may have a hard time saying as Jesus did "…they don't know what they are doing." We want to say 'yes they do, oh, yes they do.' The reality is they really don't. If they truly knew the implications, the affects physically, psychological and spiritually, especially to themselves, they wouldn't have.

4. ASK THE LORD TO FORGIVE YOU FOR YOUR UN-FORGIVENESS — Un-forgiveness is a sin…right? Oooops! We sometimes forget that, and as such it separates us from God and the things He wants to bless us with. Jesus is the model; He is the Word of God we look to, to know if we are hitting the mark. He forgave and forgave freely, to the point of dying for those who put Him on the Cross…wow! We then are to do the same. When we don't, we are not reflecting Him and we have missed the mark, we have sinned. Even this He died for, my cold and calloused heart caught in the grips of un-forgiveness.

5. PRAY BLESSING ON THE PERSON — Here is another opportunity to practice the Word of God. In Luke 6:28, Jesus says, "bless those who curse you, pray for those who mistreat you," and later He says in Luke 6:38b, "…For with the measure you use, it will be measured to you." It is here that we find the courage to do the very thing that will be as the healing balm over our wounds. That's why when I say to pray for the person who wronged you, it doesn't mean to pray those "two by four prays." The "go get them, oh Lord," or "You know they need You, oh God," type prayers. No, pray blessing and prosperity over the person. Pray for them what they took away from you. If they took relationship from you, pray that their relationships would be fulfilling and rich. If they stole from you, pray that they would prosper monetarily, and have all their needs met. With the same measure you use, it will be measured back to you…what a promise and motivation to give-away that which I am in need of, just to experience God's favor in seeing it returned back to me. In the mean time, how freeing, and what healing is experienced in putting into practice that which God has already done for me.

.

Putting it together

Keys to a prospering soul are:

1st Thanksgiving (Enter His Gates)

2nd Confession (Go to the Laver)

3rd Reconciliation (On the way to the Altar)

4th Surrender (At the Altar)

5th Forgive (Back to the Laver)

So let's do it!

Take a moment and give this fifth Key a try. Use the model given and do it with all your heart. Here is a sample of how you might start:

"Lord I need to forgive _____. Give me the strength to see your will completed in my life."

It's your turn. Write your opening prayer here and then work through the "Forgiveness model" for each person you feel you need to release."

Chapter 10: Key #6 Confidence

Intro

"Hey! Where are you going?" the nurse called to us as we burst into the CCU of our local hospital. One of our friends had been in a car accident on Sunday afternoon just after church. It was Father's Day. Some others from our church and I responded in the only way we knew how, and that was, to get in there and pray! This was not a time to think about protocol, or offending someone. We knew what we were there for and what we needed to do. Thank God for the doctors and nurses, but Janet (not her real name) needed more than that…she needed a miracle!

Our attitude in entering that CCU with conviction, determination, faith, and most of all confidence, started a series of events that ultimately lead to Janet's walking out of there six days later. She was totally healed despite her injuries which were fatally severe. Confidence is what this chapter is all about, and our main passage of scripture is found in Hebrews 10:19–23 (NIV):

> "Therefore, brothers, since we have *confidence* to enter the Most Holy Place by the blood of Jesus, [20] by a new and living way opened for us through the curtain, that is, his body, [21] and since we have a great priest over the house of God, [22] let us draw near to God with a sincere heart in full assurance of faith, having our hearts sprinkled to cleanse us from a guilty conscience and having our bodies washed with pure water. [23] Let us hold unswervingly to the hope we profess, for he who promised is faithful."

As I like to say about many verses of scripture that speak to me so profoundly, this is huge! We can't miss what the writer is saying here, though I believe this is one of those sections in the Bible that gets passed over too quickly. It is truly the point of our understanding of what God intended in laying out the Tabernacle and its regulations, and how we apply it to our own lives. Confidence leads to entering. By entering we are drawing near to God. We draw near to Him with sincere hearts, in faith, because our hearts have been cleansed from guilt, and we have experienced freedom through forgiveness and reconciliation. In short, our daily taking a walk through the Tabernacle, utilizing it as a spiritual discipline in our lives, results in confidence before God, and with this boldness to pray and expect our prayers to have the impact intended.

I won't leave you hanging concerning Janet and the circumstances surrounding her remarkable healing. The best doctors in that hospital, after looking at her X-rays, could only shake their heads and admit there was little they could do. Janet, who was pregnant and not wearing a lap belt at the time of the accident, had ruptured her spleen, her pelvis was broken in two places, and her wrist was broken. Her wrist was the only thing the hospital treated by putting a cast on it. Her embryonic sack had been punctured, allowing the fluid inside to leak and blood to go in. She did not have any head injuries, but overall, the doctors concluded they would not operate on her for fear of losing her or the baby in the process. For twenty-four hours a day, someone was in Janet's room praying and reading the Bible. On Tuesday night, Janet had a remarkable encounter with God and by Wednesday morning she was completely healed, except for her wrist which was in the cast. The hospital staff was so amazed by what happened they could scarcely believe it. They kept her there until Saturday to run tests, teach her to walk (even though she was running up and down the hallways, going outside, and visiting other patients), and they moved her for one day to a regular room, because you can't be discharged home from CCU! Her OBGYN even scheduled a C-section because of her injuries, but the Lord had her go into labor three days before the surgery, and she had the baby as she had prayed for, by natural childbirth.

      Confidence in God's ability, and our authority as His representatives was key to the miracle we saw that week, and it taught me a valuable lesson about prayer and our relationship with God…He wants us to Enter Boldly into His presence and ask Him specifically what we need. Hebrews 4:16 (NIV) says:

"Let us then approach the throne of grace with confidence, so that we may receive mercy and find grace to help us in our time of need."

The Punch Line

Every good story has a point; every joke has a punch line. It is what makes all that is being said make sense. What was the point of the Tabernacle of Moses, what was the reason for its accoutrements? Why can we use it as a model to keep our souls prospering, and a key to effective prayer? It is, to "cleanse us from a guilty conscience" so that we may "draw near to God with a sincere heart in full assurance of faith." Why, because there are things in our lives that come back at us. As Christ-followers we may know that Jesus' death on the Cross bought us forgiveness, we may know that we are ambassadors of reconciliation, we may understand that we are servants of the Most High God. Unfortunately, our experiences speak of something else. People hurt us, they hold things against us, and we don't feel worthy to serve a Holy God in His Holy quest…all because of guilt whose effect is to sap us of our confidence in approaching God. If we can't approach Him, we can't pray. If we don't pray, the things God wants to do through us and to us are hindered, delayed, and held back by unseen forces whose job it is to keep us from being effective for the Kingdom of God.

What the Tabernacle represents to me is FREEDOM! God made sure Moses understood everything about this tent and all the items to go along with it. There was such specificity. He wanted us to understand He is a part of our everyday lives, totally interested in what happens to us, and that the person of Jesus represents the fulfillment of His promise to "dwell among [His] people." He has shown us the way to healing, wholeness, and effectiveness. It resides in practicing the things laid out in the Tabernacle, not just sometimes, but each day. If we could truly live lives that are content and grateful to God; if we could truly come before Him with hands that are clean; if we could sincerely make things right between us and those close to us; if we could see our lives as His to do with as He pleases; if we could keep short accounts with people, forgiving quickly, then there would be nothing in our experiences to bring us guilt. There would be nothing the enemy would have on us to throw in our faces each time we attempted to step out and grab hold of that which God has promised. We would be as close as we possibly could be to a Jesus look-a-like; living with the same sense of freedom, exuding the same confidence He had when He said in John 14:30 NIV):

> "I will not speak with you much longer, for the prince of this world is coming. He has no hold on me...,"

In other words, this guy is coming and he is looking for something in my life to hang over my head and use against me when he needs, BUT let him come, because there is nothing, not even one thing there. We can have freedom from guilt, freedom to experience God, freedom to obey Him at any time, anywhere. Freedom to approach Him and ask for the things needed is what the punch line of this story is all about.

Enter Boldly

To enter boldly doesn't mean to enter arrogantly. The word used here in the original language is translated most as "confidence," and really has the idea of being free to speak ones mind. It's the "boldness" to say what is truly on ones heart. We can enter boldly because we know first and foremost God is the one who beckons us to come. Subsequent to that, He has made the way, through the design of the Tabernacle, for us to come running, not hesitating because of a guilty conscience and sense of unworthiness.

Entering? Entering What?

Some might say, 'Lou this is nice, but isn't this totally a Jewish/Old Testament thing, not really for we New Testament people?' Well, go back and look at the scriptures highlighting each "Key" starting with Chapter 5. Are they New or Old Testament verses? Don't bother, I'll tell you. They were all from the New Testament, save for one, the first (Psalm 100).

The significance of the Tabernacle as our model has its greatest impact when we realize what was in the Tent of Meeting. In the first room, known as the Holy Place, stood the items used in the daily worship of God. In the second room, the Holy of Holies, was the Ark of the Covenant, which represented the very Presence of God. In all, there were only four items in the Tent not including the curtain that originally separated the two rooms. As we know, when Jesus died on the Cross, that curtain was torn from top to bottom, essentially opening up the entire area, making one large room. (Matt. 27:50–51) For us, the placement of these items represents a magnificent picture of what we are entering into when we come into His presence. The Altar of Incense represents us standing before God. Incense was burned on it, signifying prayers rising up before Him, because that's what we are there to do…pray. The Table of Shewbread is Jesus, the bread of life that fell from heaven (John 6). The Lampstand is the Holy Spirit, the one who brings light to the world by revealing all that must be seen, and also the One who reveals who God is to us. Of course, the Ark of the Covenant represents God the Father, the One to whom we address in prayer. The priests of old didn't realize it, but they were standing in the midst of the Trinity, the Godhead, Elohim in all His personages. What a concept! That we, as lowly as we are, can enter into the very presence of God, seeing Him as He has revealed Himself, and there speak our minds, fully expecting that what we are asking will be granted.

Confidence is the key

Think of those times when you are most confident. They are probably times you are doing something familiar, or something repeated over and over again, and therefore you know what comes next. I would imagine they are things you don't even think about. In other words, you just do them. You may even take for granted what you do as normal for everyone as it comes so easy to you. I can remember the first time someone asked me to speak in front of a group. I died a thousand deaths from lack of confidence, particularly in my abilities from my lack of experience. I would rather have gone to the dentist, and that's saying a lot knowing how much I just don't like doing that! Not that I consider myself a great orator, but now people come up to me and comment how natural I come across as I speak. I am comfortable speaking because I have been doing it for the past 20+ years! I would still be nervous if I was asked to speak on something I was not too familiar with. I may not even take the engagement because I believe to truly be effective there's nothing like personal illustrations to back up what you're saying.

God intended us to be confident in His presence, to the point of not even thinking about anything else. He also knew that sometimes our experiences tend to put distance between what God desires for our relationship with Him and what actually happens. I've been pastoring long enough, and have counseled enough people, to know that life just gets in our way sometimes. It is great to know that God has made the way for us to overcome our deficiencies. Not only did God make the way through Jesus, who is the fulfillment of all that went before, but He took care of everything that would come after as well. He laid out for us that which would truly keep us whole, healthy, and confident.

Confidence makes us affective. It is the key to our succeeding in that which we feel called and compelled to undertake. Someone recently gave me a picture of the start of a women's marathon race. In it, you see all of the runners standing waiting for the gun to sound. Every one of them was looking off to the sides in either direction except for two who were staring ahead. They both had dark sunglasses, but one of them lowered hers so she could clearly see what was before her. Her eyes were intense as she stared down the course laid out before her, and you can actually see the sense of purpose and confidence she was exuding. Who do you think won that race? It wasn't those who were looking off to the sides distracted by the goings on around them, and it wasn't the one who kept her glasses on which gave her a distorted view of reality. It was the one who wasn't afraid to look at what was truly there, whether good or bad. She was going forward with confidence because she was given the ability to succeed. God has made the way for us to succeed. Not only through Jesus' death on the Cross which conquered both sin and death, but for us to know the reality of that victory in our daily lives by giving us a model to follow to keep us in shape, and ready to go.

Putting it together
Keys to a prospering soul are to:

1st Thanksgiving (Enter His Gates)

2nd Confession (Go to the Laver)

3rd Reconciliation (On the way to the Altar)

4th Surrender (At the Altar)

5th Forgive (Back to the Laver)

6th Confidence (Enter God's Presence Boldly)

So let's do it!

Take a moment and give this sixth Key a try. Here is a sample of how you might start:

"Lord I come to you boldly, knowing that you receive me as your (son/daughter) free from those things that have entangled my life. I know you hear my prayer because you are my Father."

It's your turn. Write a simple prayer to remind you of God's faithfulness and desire for you to be with him:

Chapter 11: Key #7 Communication

Intro

The scene is a summer day; a mother and father are both busily working about the house. Two siblings are playing together in a room. They are just two years apart in age and not more than two and four years old, respectively. All of a sudden, the eldest comes in to see dad to explain something he doesn't like his brother doing with his toys. Knowing perfectly well what he wants to say, he ventures into an attempt at accurately communicate his feelings. The words however don't seem to come out fast enough, or he just doesn't know enough of them to properly express himself. After listening to his son start his first sentence about five times, the dad patiently says, "It's ok son, just slow down. What do you want?" Again the boy tries, "Dad…dad…dad…….uh, dad." The father picks him up, looks at him intently and gently says, "Just tell me what you want." "Can...can you tell my brother to stop messing up my toys?" The father looks at him with a smile and says, "Now that wasn't so hard was it?" "Let's go see."

This may not have been your experience with your father, or it may not even accurately describe how you see yourself handling your children. I do believe it is how we approach God our Father at times. The great thing about it is He is always there to encourage us to just be specific. We often have so much we want to say, our thoughts swirl about our heads but nothing really comes out of our mouths. Too often we fill the air with lots of words, talking around issues, logically trying to assume a response, but never getting to the point.

One of the greatest influences in my life, outside of Jesus, has been a man named John Wimber. John essentially is the founder of the Vineyard movement, an international church planting movement, which has had tremendous impact to many, not only in the area of church life, but ministry, music, missions and much more. In teaching about praying for others, specifically in a ministry context, John used to point out how short the prayers of Jesus were. "See," "Be healed," "Walk," and so on. John would emphasize our authority to affect what needed to be done by being specific, just as Jesus modeled in His prayers for the sick. This has been the model I've chosen ever since I first heard it, and I believe it conveys faith, trust, acknowledgement of my position as a son of God, and most importantly, it allows me to recognize the answers to my prayers much, much easier.

In our trek through the Tabernacle, we suddenly find ourselves face to face with God. He is our Father, and the

One who can affect that which needs to be done. What do I do in this moment, what is it that I really need? Is it to hear from the Lord like Moses? Or, is it just to sit there quietly and be refreshed in His presence like Joshua, Moses' apprentice. (Exodus 33:11) I know this, I want to make the most of this opportunity and there are a few things that are immediately available to me; (1) Intercession and (2) Refreshing.

Praying to Know the Answer

Hebrews 4:16 (NIV) states:

> "Let us then approach the throne of grace with confidence, so that we may receive mercy and find grace to help us in our time of need."

The word "confidence" here is the word "parrhessia" in the original language, and when translated means to "utter-all" or "speak-all." It conveys the idea of being forthcoming or speaking plainly and specifically. Why? Because there is no time like the present to obtain that which is needed, and no one else but God who can do it for you!

There is a wonderful account in the Bible of someone who had the proper approach to their relationship with God, the boldness to stand in His Presence, and the wear-with-all to pray in such a way as to recognize the answer to their prayer when answered. It is found in Genesis 18, and it involves Abraham and his concerns for the people of Sodom and Gomorrah. We pick up the story at verse 20:

> Then the Lord said, "The outcry against Sodom and Gomorrah is so great and their sin so grievous [21] that I will go down and see if what they have done is

as bad as the outcry that has reached me. If not, I will know." [22] The men turned away and went toward Sodom, but Abraham remained standing before the Lord. [23] Then Abraham approached him and said: "Will you sweep away the righteous with the wicked? [24] What if there are fifty righteous people in the city? Will you really sweep it away and not spare the place for the sake of the fifty righteous people in it? [25] Far be it from you to do such a thing--to kill the righteous with the wicked, treating the righteous and the wicked alike. Far be it from you! Will not the Judge of all the earth do right?" [26] The Lord said, "If I find fifty righteous people in the city of Sodom, I will spare the whole place for their sake." [27] Then Abraham spoke up again: "Now that I have been so bold as to speak to the Lord, though I am nothing but dust and ashes, [28] what if the number of the righteous is five less than fifty? Will you destroy the whole city because of five people?" "If I find forty-five there," he said, "I will not destroy it." [29] Once again he spoke to him, "What if only forty are found there?" He said, "For the sake of forty, I will not do it." [30] Then he said, "May the Lord not be angry, but let me speak. What if only thirty can be found there?" He answered, "I will not do it if I find thirty there." [31] Abraham said, "Now that I have been so bold as to speak to the Lord, what if only twenty can be found there?" He said, "For the sake of twenty, I will not destroy it." [32] Then he said, "May the Lord not be angry, but let me speak just once more. What if only ten can be found there?" He answered, "For the

> sake of ten, I will not destroy it." [33] When the Lord had finished speaking with Abraham, he left, and Abraham returned home.

In being allowed to look into this intimate encounter between Abraham and God, we must not presume that God doesn't already know the state of the people of those two cities. If God:

> "...knows the thoughts of man; [and] knows that they are futile." Psalm 94:11 (NIV)
>
> "...know[s] when I sit and when I rise; [and] perceive[s] my thoughts from afar. Psalm 139:2 (NIV)
>
> "...detests the thoughts of the wicked, but those of the pure are pleasing to him. Proverbs 15:26 (NIV)

...he didn't have to go physically to these cities to "see" what the people were up to, He already knew what was in their hearts. However, Abraham didn't know and he was concerned, so he approached God to find out. God didn't stop Abraham in his tracks or tell him 'it's none of your business,' He listened and answered each question. The question Abraham had was, "will you sweep away the righteous with the wicked?" It's a good question and a valid prayer because it came out of a sincere heart for others and their condition. What we have to recognize here is that Abraham's reverence for the Lord was just as important as the actual prays he prayed. He knew that God was not one to act in an unrighteous manner by dealing with the wicked and the righteous the same. So Abraham comes humbly before the Lord, yet boldly, and asks specifically about a number of righteous people that the Lord would consider too many to destroy the entire place. He continues to reduce the number becoming more specific as he goes along to satisfy his own thoughts in the matter until it says God was done and He left. In other words, when God became silent about the matter, Abraham was done asking Him about it and waited to see what would happen. The final answer came of course:

> "Early the next morning Abraham got up and returned to the place where he had stood before the Lord. [28] He looked down toward Sodom and Gomorrah, toward all the land of the plain, and he saw dense smoke rising from the land, like smoke from a furnace. Genesis 19:27–28 (NIV)

No direct conversation was needed in the form of continued questioning from Abraham, the answer was right before his eyes. He was specific enough, and the Lord gracious enough to give him the answer he was looking for. Those two cities were in bad shape, even worse than possibly Abraham had first thought, but he wouldn't have known that unless he had asked. He sought the Lord, and he found the Lord. He was specific in his query and he didn't have to go looking for the answer, the answer found him.

Intercession is not the only thing immediately available to us as we find ourselves in the presence of the Lord.

Times of Refreshing

I often find myself pointing out to some that when we speak of the "Lord's Presence," or "being in the Presence of the Lord," that we shouldn't fall into the trap of relegating the experience to "it" status. In other words, we must realize that the "Lord's Presence" *is* the Lord. Moses understood this because of his experiences with God in and out of the Tabernacle. Let's look at one of them in Exodus 33:11–20 (NIV) [words in bold are the same Hebrew word "panyim," and is mostly translated as "presence" or "face" and denotes the idea of a frontal view, or being before someone or something]:

> "The Lord would speak to Moses **face** to **face**, as a man speaks with his friend. Then Moses would return to the camp, but his young aide Joshua son of Nun did not leave the tent. [12] Moses said to the Lord, "You have been telling me, 'Lead these people,' but you have not let me know whom you will send with me. You have said, 'I know you by name and you have found favor with me.' [13] If you are pleased with me, teach me your ways so I may know you and continue to find favor with you. Remember that this nation is your people." [14] The Lord replied, "My **Presence** will go with you, and I will give you rest." [15] Then Moses said to him, "If your **Presence** does not go with us, do not send us up from here. [16] How will anyone know that you are pleased with me and with your people unless you go with us? What else will distinguish me and your people from all the other people on the **face** of the

earth?" [17] And the Lord said to Moses, "I will do the very thing you have asked, because I am pleased with you and I know you by name." [18] Then Moses said, "Now show me your glory." [19] And the Lord said, "I will cause all my goodness to pass in **front** of you, and I will proclaim my name, the Lord, in your **presence**. I will have mercy on whom I will have mercy, and I will have compassion on whom I will have compassion. [20] But," he said, "you cannot see my **face**, for no one may see me and live."" (Bold lettering is mine)

Without getting too deep theologically, there is one thing that is made clear here, God's Presence is God Himself, and He tells Moses in verse fourteen that with His Presence comes "rest." As a matter of fact, God in reply to Moses' inquiry as to "whom [God] will send with [him]," in essence says, 'you don't need anyone else to go with you…I, the Lord, will go with you and I'm all you need.' So therefore, Moses could "rest," or at least find rest in the fact that God's Presence would be with him. One final point from this passage we mustn't miss, and that is, God's Presence was tangibly recognizable. Moses knew when God's Presence was there and when He was not. Moses knew others would be able to tell as well, so it wasn't some secret or perceived Presence, there was an actual manifested reality of experience, and that is what he expected to find, whether that was in-person or through fulfilled promises. For Moses it was both!

What does that have to do with us? Look at Acts 3:19 (NKJV)

> "Repent therefore and be converted, that your sins may be blotted out, so that times of refreshing may come from the **presence** of the Lord…"

Peter spoke these words to those who were astonished at the healing of a lame man. He took the opportunity to witness to them and tell them how to be saved. The word for presence here is the Greek equivalent to that found in the Exodus passage. Simply he said, 'reconsider what you think you know, and the direction you are heading, and follow Jesus. By doing this, you will turn to the right way which will obliterate all those things you do which go against God and don't represent Him. When you do this, you will be *revived* because you will "see" the Lord. He will become apparent to you.'

Our souls prosper when we practice and put into our lives as a spiritual discipline, the continual turning back to the Lord. Sin separates us from the Lord's Presence, but He gives us the way back each time…just take a walk through the Tabernacle. The Tabernacle has every element needed for your souls to prosper. Whether that is an attitude of a grateful heart, the need for forgiveness of your sins, reconciliation with others, the laying down of your life to the service of the Lord, or releasing others for the wrongs they have done to you. The Lord knows we need to practice these things everyday. As His sons and daughters, our experiences in living this life should equal our position as a member of His family. The Tabernacle reminds us of the way in, especially when we lose our way. It is the road map through the confusing and often frustrating terrain of life's ups and downs.

The role of the Intercessor

Before leaving this section, I feel it is necessary to give a short brief on the role of the Intercessor. In speaking of making the most of the opportunity, and in light of the passage we utilized in Exodus 33:11–20, we cannot miss the fact that Moses was *interceding* on behalf of the people. To intercede simply means "to be in the position of obtaining." It doesn't require prayer as in the case of Jesus who,

> "...is able to save completely those who come to God through him, because he always lives to **intercede** for them." (Hebrews 7:25) (NIV)

He does this of course through His finished work on the Cross. However, it is mostly associated with some sort of petition on behalf or against people, as in the case of Elijah, as Paul points out, "God did not reject his people, whom he foreknew. Don't you know what the Scripture says in the passage about Elijah—how he **appealed** [interceded] to God against Israel." (Romans 11:2) (Bold lettering and bracketed addition are mine]

This is in reference to the account found in 1 Kings 19:10–18, when Elijah thought he was the only one left serving God in Israel.

The point is that there is a relationship between God's position as King over all creation, man's position as His delegates, and His working in and through man to affect His creation. That affecting is what we call Intercession. As the leader of the Hebrew people, one of Moses' roles was to intercede, be the go-between, to obtain that which was required to affect God's will. God uses people, and in this case, Moses.

God will use you as well! As members of His body, and ones who have complete access to God "...through the curtain which is His [Jesus'] body...," (Hebrews 10:20) [Bracketed addition mine] we find ourselves in the same position as Moses. Not in the sense of being a leader, with its responsibility and accountability, but as ones who have been called near to God. This is a unique privilege, and at that time, we find we are in the role of the intercessor. This, to either pray and petition God, or to be instructed by Him to accomplish some task which will help in affecting His Kingdom's work here on earth. Intercession then is not just for a few "gifted" individuals who lock themselves in their "prayer closets" to petition God and do spiritual warfare. Those things are part of it, but not all of it. Intercession is the position we find ourselves in, in our relationship to God, at a time and place where we are communicating with Him, or fulfilling that which He has commanded us to do on His behalf.

Putting it together

Keys to a prospering soul are:

1st Thanksgiving (Enter His Gates)

2nd Confession (Go to the Laver)

3rd Reconciliation (On the way to the Altar)

4th Surrender (At the Altar)

5th Forgive (Back to the Laver)

6th Confidence (Enter God's Presence Boldly)

7th Communicate (Intimate Conversation)

So let's do it!

Take a moment and give this seventh Key a try. Here is a sample of how you might start:

"Lord I'm asking for your help with _____. I know you are with me so I pray that _____ will be resolved. Bless my family and pour out your Spirit upon them. Help _____ with all they are going through. Heal _____ from their illness and bring salvation to _____."

It's your turn. Write some of your personal prayers here and know that God will answer you:

Chapter 12: Working It In And Out

Intro

Someone once told me Alfred Adler, the famous psychologist, once put an ad in the paper for a Fourteen-Day Cure Plan. He claimed that he could cure anyone of any mental or emotional difficulty in just fourteen days if they would do just what he told them to do.

One day, a woman who was extremely lonely came to see Adler. He told her he could cure her of her loneliness in just fourteen days if she would follow his advice. She was not impressed, but she still asked, 'What do you want me to do?' Adler replied, 'If you will do something for someone else everyday for fourteen days, at the end of that time, your loneliness will go away.'

She profusely objected, 'Why should I do anything for someone else? No one ever does anything for me.' Adler supposedly responded jokingly, 'Well, maybe it will take you twenty-one days.'

If there is one thing that is painfully obvious in presenting the material of this book, it is that without a heart to see it through, and worked out in our lives on a consistent basis, it will do little good to the reader. The Keys presented here, and the use of the Tabernacle of Moses as a visual model, can only act as helpful tools for a prospering soul in the constant practice of them.

Alfred Adler recognized that everyone is not the same. What one person can do in fourteen days may take someone else twenty-one. Habits, or in our case, "spiritual disciplines" need to be put into our lives which promote the outcome we desire.

I've heard that Tom Landry said, "the job of a football coach is to make men do what they don't want to do, in order to achieve what they've always wanted to be." In other words, some things don't come naturally to us, so we don't really have a heart to do them, especially if there is some perceived hardship or difficulty associated with it. As a former high school football player, I experienced those hardships. Practicing in the heat of a New York August day with pads on, running "wind sprints" up a hill at the end of practice, was not a thing to look forward to the next day, yet we showed up day after day. Why? We loved the game, and we knew that when it came to competing in an actual game, to achieve the edge required for victory, we had to be in shape.

As believers who pray for revival to come to our world, our country, and our locale, we must be willing to "pay the price," to achieve that which we so desire, and it must start with us. It does no good for a football team to say it wants to win, when the individuals on that team make no effort to be at their best in order to achieve that victory.

Individually we *can* all experience a prospering soul. The closeness and effectiveness we all pray for, in our church, our community and the world are realized when we understand it starts with us.

The Tabernacle, and the accoutrements within it, is like a football practice field. The items inside it are like the various machines and drill component apparatus deemed necessary by the coach for the players' benefit. The love for our coach, Jesus, is motivation enough to move us from practice component to practice component in order to get ready for the competition, which is, the battle between the Kingdom of God and the Kingdom of Satan.

So let's look at how we might approach implementing the Elements of a Prosperous Soul as described in this book, recognizing that not everyone is the same, and it's not the letter of the law that's important, but rather the outcome.

Desiring to Desire

Ramsey MacDonald was once the Prime Minister of England, and he was discussing with another government official the possibility of lasting peace. The government official, who was an expert on foreign affairs, was supposedly unimpressed by the Prime Minister's idealistic point of view. He remarked with cynicism that the desire for peace does not necessarily ensure it. MacDonald admitted this could be the case, adding that neither does the desire for food satisfy your hunger. At least that gets you started toward a restaurant.

God will meet you where you are! We've heard that said many times, and I'm sure many of us have even said that to others at times as well. The desire for something is the starting place. It is the proverbial "crossing over the line," to actually obtaining that which is desired, but for some of us, we need to desire to desire. If MacDonald was literally talking about hunger, he would say, 'we need to be hungry for hunger.'

For those who have a desire to see God moving more powerfully in their lives already, you will undoubtedly, as long as you see the benefit from it, assimilate the Keys presented here without delay. You are the ones who are hungry for God and hungry to see your souls prospering. You are already in the place necessary to activate a prayer life that has greater and more effective impact upon your world. Yet for some, you need to come to a place that desires such things. "God *will* meet you where you are."

So...where are you? You must answer this question before you attempt to jump into appropriating the benefits associated with the ordinances of the Tabernacle. I know, I know...our present day world doesn't have patience enough to work through something in order to reap a benefit later on, but it is the reality of it. Desire must be instilled in your heart in order to mix in the Keys of the Tabernacle. Then, and only then, will you not only start, but you will continue for *years* to come to walk through the Tabernacle just as you take a walk through your house or apartment. It will become as natural a part of your day as putting on your clothes.

Legalism vs. Liberty

Have you ever gone to a conference or listened to a speaker talk about a certain topic of interest to you, and the reason you paid the money to be there was because you knew that person has authority in the subject matter? They talk about their success stories and the like, and you get pumped-up to go home and try it. That pumped-up feeling often lasts as long as you're first and if you're really committed possibly your second attempt at doing just as the presenter laid it out. Reconciling that person's success with the truths they are promoting is the difference needed to assimilate the benefits to your life. There is a principle, a key element being addressed, yet the package, or interpretation and contextualization of the material has us looking at it instead of what God is truly trying to say. That is the difference between legalism and liberty.

Legalism says you must do something a certain way or you're a failure; you're less a Christian then those who have attained to the higher reaches....nirvana! NO! Please don't go there with the Keys presented here. There is benefit, yes, there is model, yes, but the individual Keys or principles themselves have eternal benefits all their own. Must you use the Tabernacle as *your* model? Not if it doesn't do it for you. Use anything that gets you to appropriate the distinctive associated with the Tabernacle, and utilized by the New Testament writers, but just do it. Whether you do them all at once, in one prayer/devotional time, or split them up and do different Keys on different days, it doesn't really matter, so long as you "Come to God with a Grateful Heart," so long as you "Confess your sins regularly," so long as you "Reconcile yourself with others," so long a you "Lay down your life to the service of the Lord," so long as you Forgive those who have wronged you," and so long as you know you are welcomed and can "Enter Boldly" into the Lord's Presence. What matters is that it happens. If it is truly happening, you are happening! There is liberty in the material presented here. Models have their place, so long as they don't confuse and cloud over the point of the exercise.

One other point on this topic; there is a tendency to go "overboard" on anything new to us. Not in the sense of having enthusiasm and zeal for the Lord and growing closer to Him, but in the expectations we have of ourselves, and the time frame we give ourselves to get there. You've heard it said I'm sure, that the only way to eat an elephant is "one bite at a time." Know who you are and how you either put too much or not enough pressure on yourself. Do you have too high or too low an expectation of your own accomplishments? Look at the successes in your own life, as well as the failures, and see if you can see an attitude difference. What is it that drives you to continue in something and what is that makes you drop something, even those things that are good for you? Pace yourself! Are you one who needs to get right in there and start doing something like these Keys, utilizing the model of the

Tabernacle every day? Then do it. If it is better for you to take it slow and give it a try at first, and then let it lie for a short while, then do it. There is something to be said for consistency, especially for the things associated here, but consistency could be everyday to some, and once a week for others. I would simply say, 'do it at a pace that promotes long-term practice.' Joggers know that there is a regimen that, depending on who they are, elicits burnout or atrophy. Too much, too soon, and we don't ever want to do it again. Too little, too spaced apart, and we can become apathetic and flabby.

Some practical considerations

As someone who has been taking a walk through the Tabernacle for many years now, I recognize there is a difference now than when I first began. When I first started, I can remember I wouldn't get passed "The Gate" of the Tabernacle for almost fifteen or more minutes. I would just want to thank and praise God all day because of His goodness. I would then get as far as "The Laver," and because I hadn't done it for some time, it would take me my entire prayer time just to confess my sins. To tell you the truth…it took me days, but don't tell anyone! When I finally felt I could move on, I began to remember all the people that had something against me…what a bummer that was! That took me a while, I can tell you. I was not discouraged however, but determined to go on. I wanted to get to the place where my lists were short. Thank God for the "Surrendering My Life at the Altar" segment, it seemed I could get through that easy enough and at least I felt I was getting somewhere more quickly. The problem was I had to go back to the Laver, and start to forgive others for hurting me in some way. That took some time/days. When I realized I was finished with my walk, and I was ready to "Enter Boldly into the Lord's Presence," though I had done that before, and knew that I could "theologically," there was such a sense of relief and freedom this time. I was entering from not only the "positional" or theoretical point of view, but with an "experiential" and practical approach that put me in another state of mind. I knew I was living out, to the best of my ability, "ascending the hill of the Lord...[with] clean hands and a pure heart." (Ps. 24) I knew that along with being accepted because of the Sacrifice of Jesus, I was applying those things won for me at the Cross, along with the benefits to me, *and* affecting those around me all at the same time.

In applying these Keys, remember if you keep up with them, and put the model of the Tabernacle into your devotional life as a believer, you may get bogged down in one or more of the Keys because of the situations in your life, but it is just for a time. There is healing going on in your heart, and it is affecting the world around you. As time passes, you will find that your walk through the Tabernacle is steadier and somewhat predictable. It may be, because you have really used it as a spiritual discipline, that it only takes a couple of minutes. Your lists are short, and some even non-existent. Your devotional time is filled instead with more praise, thanksgiving, intercession and hearing the voice of God.

This is my prayer for you, that you would find complete freedom in your life, such that the enemy has nothing on you. You are refreshed and filled with the Lord's Presence in your life, ministering to others from the overflow of your relationship with God. That you prosper in all things, even as your soul is prospering.

__Appendix One__

Keys to Praying Through the Tabernacle

Key 1 (Enter through the Gate)

Psalm 100:4 "Enter His gates with thanksgiving and His courts with praise; give thanks to God and praise His name." We come humbly as a grateful, loving child who understands the Grace given to him/her because of what Jesus has done.

Key 2 (Go to the Laver)

1 John 1:9 "If we **confess our sins,** he is faithful and just to forgive us our sins and cleanse us from all unrighteousness." The priest would wash in the Laver as a sign of cleansing, a purification. We simply confess our sins, say the same thing God is saying about it, and apply the purifying work of the Word of God in our lives.

Key 3 (While on the way to the Altar)

Matthew 5:23-24 "Therefore, if you are offering your gift at the altar and there remember that your brother has something against you, leave your gift there at the altar. First go and **be reconciled** to your brother, then come and offer your gift." The word "reconcile" here means "to make it different." Remember it says if your brother has something against you, not you have something against your brother. Also remember, "as far as it is with you"; you cannot dictate the actions of another.

Key 4 (Go to the Altar)

Romans 12:1 "Therefore, I urge you, brothers, in view of God's mercy, to **offer your bodies as living sacrifices**, holy and pleasing to God-this is your spiritual act of worship." At this point we come to the altar and make our sacrifice. No longer do we use animals or anything else, now we offer ourselves, our lives laid down for God's purposes.

Key 5 (Back to the Laver)

Mark 11:25 "And when you stand praying, if you hold anything against anyone, **forgive** him, so that your Father in heaven may forgive you your sins." We no longer go to the Laver to wash off blood, now we go to apply the Blood of Christ in extending forgiveness to those who have wronged us just as we ourselves have applied it on our behalf.

Key 6 (Enter the Holy Place)

Hebrews 10:17-23 "Their sins and their lawless deeds I will remember no more. And where these have been forgiven, there is no longer any sacrifice for sin. Therefore, brothers, **since we have confidence to enter the Most Holy Place** by the blood of Jesus, by a new a living way opened for us through the curtain, that is, His body and since we have a great priest over the hose of God, let us draw near to God with a sincere heart in full assurance of faith, having our heart sprinkled to cleanse us from a guilty conscience and having our bodies washed with pure water. Let us hold unswervingly to the hope we profess, for He who promised is faithful." Enter with confidence!!

Key 7 (Intimate Communication)

Hebrews 4:16 "Let us then approach the throne of grace with confidence, so that we may receive mercy and find grace to help us in our time of need." In the Lord's presence we find refreshing, help, and direction. **It's here that we commune and communicate with God** in an intimate way knowing He knows us better than we know ourselves.

Appendix Two

The Layout and Placement of Items inside the Tabernacle

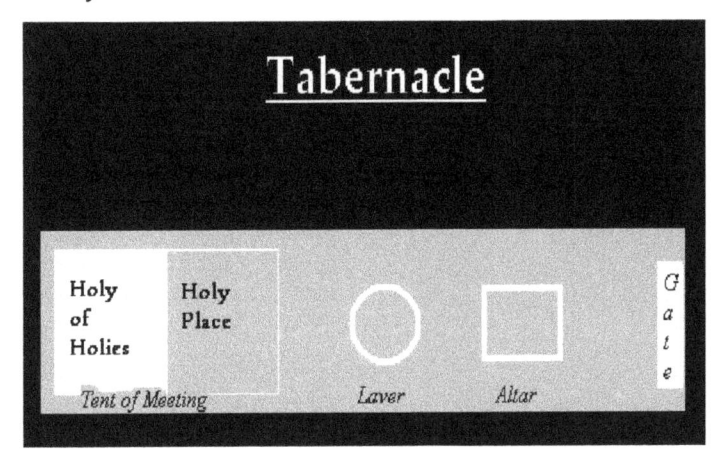

Tabernacle

| Holy of Holies | Holy Place | | Laver | Altar | Gate |

Tent of Meeting

This is the model for our walk through the Tabernacle...first through the entrance, then to the Laver, next to the Altar, back to the Laver and then into the Tent of Meeting to pray.

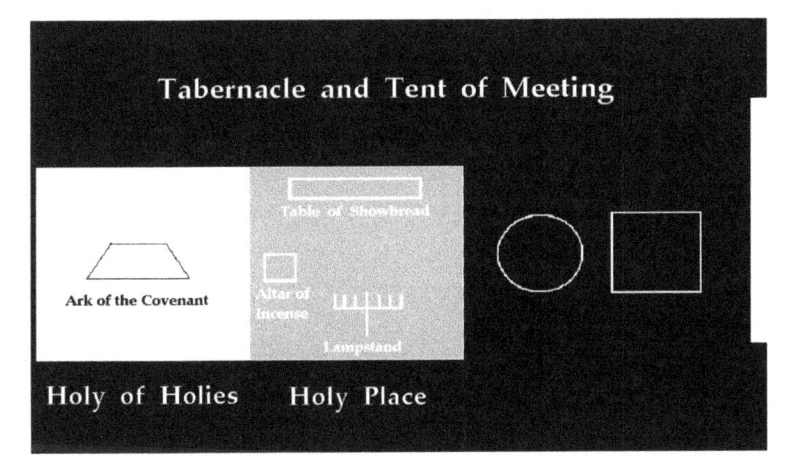

Tabernacle and Tent of Meeting

Ark of the Covenant | Table of Showbread, Altar of Incense, Lampstand

Holy of Holies | Holy Place

This is the inside of the Tent of Meeting where the priest made prayers on behalf of the people. This represents God the Father (Ark), God the Son (Showbread), God the Holy

Spirit (Menorah), and we in the midst of the Trinity praying at the Altar of Incense.

Appendix Three

The Fifteen Minute Hour

If you are just getting started in trying to spend an hour a day with the Lord, I suggest you be quite "legalistic" about the time allotments at first. Start and finish each fifteen minutes on time and move onto the next. You will find that it goes much quicker than you would ever think, and you will get more done, in terms of your spiritual life than you would ever imagine could happen in one hour!)

First Fifteen Minutes: Spend this time in Bible reading and reflection. Use it in such a way as to realize that God is speaking to you directly through His Word.

Second Fifteen Minutes: Take a walk through the Tabernacle and apply its "Keys" for a healthy Christian life. Utilize worship music, or sing to the Lord as you start.

Third Fifteen Minutes: This can be a time to "Be still before the Lord" in quite reflection and listening. Pray in the Spirit (tongues), if you utilize this spiritual gift. If you are uncomfortable with this, try reading a devotional book that will help you draw closer to the Lord. Journal through your impressions, prayers and momentary reflections as a tool to help you remember what God is showing you.

Last Fifteen Minutes: Pray for your family, friends and neighbors. Bless them and intercede for them. Make a list and start with your immediate family and work your way through your extended relations. Then move onto those who have asked you to pray for them about something.

Appendix Four

Five Steps of Forgiveness

1. **EMPTY THE GARBAGE CAN** —We are like human garbage compactors… someone hurts us and we stuff it, someone else hurts us and we stuff that, and again someone else wrongs us in another way and we do the same. We do this until the time when our can gets so full that seemingly some very small and insignificant event makes the whole thing spill over, and God help the person who happens to be there when it does. What a mess, and unfortunately, what a clean up is needed. The remedy? Empty the can when it has something in it. Even with small amounts of garbage, if left there long enough it starts to smell, and you don't want to smell bad do you? The way we do this is simple. At a time alone, preferably during a quite time with the Lord while walking through the Tabernacle, we will speak to the person who wronged us, just as if they were there, telling them all they have done to us. This may take two seconds or two hours, but whatever the case, we do it until we have gotten out that which we need to.

2. **SPEAK OUT FORGIVENSS FROM THE HEART** — Once we have spoken out the wrong(s) done to us, as best we can, from our hearts, we say something like, 'Even though you have done this to me, I forgive you.' This is only the second step however, and there's three more to go….hmmmm, I wonder why?

3. ASK THE LORD TO FORGIVE THE PERSON — Jesus, while hanging on the Cross, gave us a wonderful example of forgiveness when He said, "Father forgive them, they don't know what they are doing." (Luke 23:34) This is important for a couple of reasons: (a) It is a recognition of the relationship between myself and God, and truly whatever I bind on earth, will be bound in heaven. (b) It is like a test step. I have found people who don't want God to forgive, they want Him to remember. 'Vengeance is yours Lord, vengeance is yours!' All of a sudden they are Old Testaments scholars. They may start quoting some of their favorite Psalms, which in a paraphrase may say something like, 'Rip their eyes out, oh God, ... pull out their toe nails my Rock and my Redeemer,' something like that. Unfortunately, I don't believe that's what Jesus had in mind. What we are supposed to be doing is asking God to release them from the wrongs they have done to us, even though we may have a hard time saying as Jesus did "...they don't know what they are doing." We want to say 'yes they do, oh, yes they do.' The reality is they really don't. If they truly knew the implications, the affects physically, psychological and spiritually, especially to themselves, they wouldn't have.

4. ASK THE LORD TO FORGIVE YOU FOR YOUR UN-FORGIVENESS — Un-forgiveness is a sin...right? Oooops! We sometimes forget that, and as such it separates us from God and the things He wants to bless us with. Jesus is the model; He is the Word of God we look to, to know if we are hitting the mark. He forgave and forgave freely, to the point of dying for those who put Him on the Cross...wow! We then are to do the same. When we don't, we are not reflecting Him and we have missed the mark, we have sinned. Even this He died for, my cold and calloused heart caught in the grips of un-forgiveness.

5. **PRAY BLESSING ON THE PERSON** — Here is another opportunity to practice the Word of God. In Luke 6:28, Jesus says, "bless those who curse you, pray for those who mistreat you," and later He says in Luke 6:38b, "...For with the measure you use, it will be measured to you." It is here that we find the courage to do the very thing that will be as the healing balm over our wounds. That's why when I say to pray for the person who wronged you, it doesn't mean to pray those "two by four prays." The "go get them, oh Lord," or "You know they need You, oh God," type prayers. No, pray blessing and prosperity over the person. Pray for them what they took away from you. If they took relationship from you, pray that their relationships would be fulfilling and rich. If they stole from you, pray that they would prosper monetarily, and have all their needs met. With the same measure you use, it will be measured back to you…what a promise and motivation to give-away that which I am in need of, just to experience God's favor in seeing it returned back to me. In the mean time, how freeing, and what healing is experienced in putting into practice that which God has already done for me.

Bibliography

Chapter 3
[1] Sermon Illustrations
http://www.sermonillustrations.com/a-z/p/prayer_unanswered.htm
[2] Michael Hodgin, 1001 Humorous Illustrations For Public Speaking (Zondervan Publishing House, 1994)

Chapter 4
[1-4] Theodore H. Epp, Portraits of Christ in the Tabernacle (Back to the Bible Publishers, 1979)

Chapter 7
[1] Sermon Illustrations
http://www.sermonillustrations.com/a-z/r/reconciliation.htm

Chapter 8
[1] Sermon Illustrations
http://www.sermonillustrations.com/a-z/d/death.htm
[2] Sermon Illustrations
http://www.sermonillustrations.com/a-z/f/fourth_of_july.htm